The Hiring Committee
12 Secrets of the Interviewing Process Revealed

By C. Edwin Gill
Published by GudeJob.com

THE HIRING COMMITTEE

12 Secrets of the
Interviewing Process
Revealed

C. EDWIN GILL

I0492358

The Hiring Committee
12 Secrets of the Interviewing Process Revealed

Adherence to all applicable laws and regulations, including international, federal, state, and local governing professional licensing, business practices, advertising, and all other aspects of doing business in the United States, Canada, or any other jurisdiction, is the sole responsibility of the purchaser or reader.

Please note that throughout this book I use URL shorteners from Bitly.com, which makes it easier for you to type in a link that I reference in this book instead of having to type in the full link, which often is very long. You will see URL shorteners displayed like this: **/HIRING##** (case sensitive). This means that you would type in **bit.ly/HIRING##** in the address bar to bring up the link that I reference to. Please note that this reference is primarily for those of you who purchased the softcover book instead of reading this as an ebook. For those of you who have an ebook, you can still type in the URL shortener in the address bar, but I have also provided the link so you can click in it directly to go to the page.

I need to just say that on occasion I have found that URL shorteners will sometimes take a while to load a page. I use to use the Bit.do URL shortener, but I received too much negative feedback about links not working or links taking a long time to load the page.

I had planned to migrate all the shortened links in the book to Google's URL shortener, but as of the writing of this update, Google has stated that they will be "turning down" their support for this feature.

If you have any problems with any links in the book, I would appreciate you sending me a note about is at: ed@gudejob.com. The first three persons finding five (5) or more broken links in the book will receive a free resume review from me. Just send me an email.

Thanks.

Who this book is for...

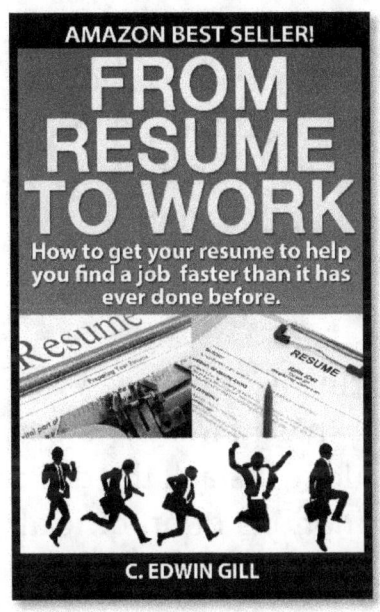

In my book, _From Resume to Work_ (/FRTW-Book), I walk you through 12 points on how your resume can get you to the hiring process for the job that you want. In this book, _The Hiring Committee,_ I share with you 12 secrets on how you can successfully navigate through the hiring process.

There's a ton of advice on the internet about how to handle an interview. In today's market, Hiring Committees are savvy in knowing that since you have access to all that information over the internet, they need to use different techniques to screen people out of their interviewing process.

What will set you apart from everyone else? That's what this book is about. The Hiring Committee will reveal 12 secrets of the hiring process from the inside. The interesting thing about this book is that it takes place during an actual hiring process.

Does a Hiring Committee really have secrets? Of course they do. Even if it is a Hiring Committee made up of a single person. This book reveals these secrets and unlocks resources for you to employ during your very next interview.

I wrote this book from my experience of hiring a Project Manager through the Hiring Committee process. As a Director, I had the perfect candidate in mind and thought I could just hire him outright like other Directors had done for their projects, but the owner of the company decided to put my hire through the Hiring Committee process. And not only that, the owner put all the other Directors on the committee, something that had never been done before.

I therefore decided that the Hiring Committee was going to be perfunctory, meaning that I already knew who I wanted for the job so I would just stack the deck in his favor and go through the motions of an official process and in the end have who I wanted in the first place.

But along the way I discovered something compelling about the Hiring Committee process — 12 secrets that every candidate who goes through the hiring process should employ in order to stack the deck in their favor.

This book is for everyone who will one day interview for a job and for everyone else who likes a good story.

Your Free Gift

I have written this report, How To Become More Valuable, in response to all of the success gurus from Steve Jobs, Napoleon Hill, Norman Vincent Peale, Robert Kiyosaki, Tony Robbins, Stephen Covey, Sharon Lechter, Neil Patel, and Les Brown, who say that you need to add value in order to succeed.

When it comes to doing a great job in an interview, how do you actually add value so that you can be more valuable to your next employer?

In this free report I will share with you why being valuable is so important (if it isn't important to you already), and how you can go about adding value to others thereby increasing your own value.

In this report I discuss seven areas where I helped job information center participants increase their value:

- **Company** – Getting a job or a better job.
- **Entrepreneurship** – Owning your own business, including such areas as construction, handyman, work-at-home person, medical field, lawyer,

vendor, store owner, or any area where you make the decisions.

- **Ebooks** – Amazon Kindle, for example.
- **Online store** – Amazon, Ebay, Shopify, etc.
- **Freelancing** – Online entrepreneur.
- **Affiliate Marketing** – Selling someone else's product online and receiving a commission.
- **Digital Marketing** – creating your own training or course and selling it online.

In each of these areas, participants were given the tools that they needed to add value to others so that they would increase their own value.

Now you can begin the process of understanding how to increase your value by adding value to others. It is my gift to you to thank you for your purchase. To get this report simply click here:

<u>/More-Valuable</u>

...or put **bit.ly/More-Valuable** in the URL address bar in your web browser.

Thanks again, and have a great day!

Case Study Video

Five people were fired on the same day, but only one of them did something that got them back on their feet with a better job in less than 30 days.

Take a moment to watch this video and to see how one person, using the right tools, turned a tragic experience into a personal triumph.

It's an inspiring story that in less than five minutes will help you to see that if you had a 10-point, 30-day action plan, it will help relieve your stress about any future job transition that every one of us must face.

You can see the video here: **/HIRING20**

| **The Hiring Committee**

Table of Contents

I NEEDED A PROJECT MANAGER

The company was ramping up its ecommerce division and I needed a Project Manager to help successfully launch this project within a certain timeline. I had the perfect person in mind so I went to Ralph, the company's president and my direct report, stated my case and provided him with the documented justification for the hire.

"Great," Ralph said, "but put it out to the committee."

I was taken aback because this wasn't Ralph's style. He usually has a *whatever it takes* attitude and allows directors like myself the autonomy to get the job done.

"I could do that," I said, "but are you sure you want to delay the work needed on the project just to go through the process, if there is a candidate already in mind?"

"I understand," he said, "but I'd like to put more eyes on this process to make sure everyone has buy-in. I'll tell you what: you chair the committee and put all the department directors together. Whoever makes it through this process, that's who we'll go with."

"Okay," I said without batting an eye, but in my mind I wondered what in the hell was going on. Every effective Hiring Committee at our company consisted of the Director, a direct report or co-worker, and sometimes someone from Human Resources. That was it. We never had a committee made up entirely of all department directors. It was just never done. And it seemed counterproductive to have myself and four other department heads, all with our own agendas, to efficiently and effectively carve out time in our busy schedules to select one person to coordinate this very important project.

I sat in my office wondering what Ralph was up to. Was he aware of how much human resources this was going to eat up when I had the perfect person in mind? Of course he was aware. Was this a scientific experiment like Frankenstein, trying to make a complete, functioning human being out of various body parts? I wasn't sure.

Ralph was almost 70 and on the verge of retiring. He had envisioned handing the business over to his two sons, but they didn't want any part of it, so one of them chose to coach a football team, while the other opened up a coffee shop. That meant Ralph would be looking for a successor within the company or to outright sell it, which was one of the projects I was working on with Generational Equity.

I could only assume that this was some type of test, either for me or for someone on the committee, so that Ralph would see what would happen. Like most companies, there were political undertones where people only embraced you so far as you could further their own agenda. I found working with each of them had its own set of challenges, so getting them together for a Hiring Committee would prove interesting at best.

I sat in my office trying to figure out if it would be better to pull the hiring request rather than go through what I thought would be a painful committee. I could have just kicked myself because all the other department heads — Gail, Mariano, Becky, and Marshall — simply hired who they needed and then provided justification afterwards. I would walk into a meeting and ta-da, I was introduced to someone new on their team. I should have listened to my friend's advice. As a manager for Comcast, Majett would often tell me, "It's easier to get forgiveness than it is to get cooperation." I didn't do that so now I had to take my perfect person through a Hiring Committee.

But I knew that projects would begin to fall through the cracks, which would require me giving up my nights and weekends again. I decided that the best thing that I could do would be to speed up the process. I would tailor the entire hiring process that my perfect candidate, Jeff, would be hired quickly and easily.

I made up my mind to design the entire hiring process around Jeff and bend the Hiring Committee's decision to where they were compelled to hire him no questions asked. And although I had completed hundreds of committee hires, I had never tried to rig one before — well, not to this extent.

I decided to help the committee out by creating this façade in which it would appear that we were going through the hiring process. I decided to do this not so much because I was not happy about going through the process, but more so that I could shorten the selection process and get back to finishing the project I was working on. In my mind, I was actually doing the committee members a favor by requiring less of their time.

I returned to my office and sat at my desk contemplating what I needed to do and why I was going to do it. I personally despise politics in the office and elsewhere because when I do it, and I have to do it every day, I feel like a chameleon trying to hide in a bag of Skittles. If I was going to submit Jeff into the fray the right way, I knew that I had to kiss a lot of butt, swallow a lot of pride, and stroke a lot of egomaniacal egos.

I also decided to use my position as the Hiring Committee Chair to accomplish a dual purpose: 1) Supply Jeff with a complete framework of the Hiring Committee process—why we hire and how he can position himself as the best candidate; and 2) Document for myself the nuances and idiosyncrasies that make up the Hiring Committee so that I would have a strategic advantage if Ralph decides to make this Hiring Committee a regular practice. I wanted to be ahead of the game.

The Hiring Committee

To achieve my dual purpose, I started by assessing the Hiring Committee. I needed to understand what hurdles I might face in order to get Jeff hired.

Let's see…

Marshall, Chief of Staff. Marshall has been Ralph's right-hand man for almost two decades. He helped Ralph build the company from a fledging business to the multi-million-dollar enterprise that it is today. Marshall is indebted to Ralph for helping him move from Burma where he was a dentist (yes, a dentist), to giving him a chance to work for an American company and to rise to the status of Chief of Staff. Marshall feels that he is Ralph's gatekeeper and his job is to shield Ralph from employees who might be detrimental to his business.

Gail, Client Relationship Director. Gail and Ralph have known each other for over 30 years. Ralph met Gail at a former company where he was a VP and she a manager. Gail came to work for Ralph's company after he suffered a stroke and needed someone he could count on other than Marshall. She seems to be the only director who has the balls to directly challenge Ralph on some of his ideas, instead of dancing around him like the rest of us do. Their arguments remind me of an entrenched married couple, and some have hinted that their relationship might tip-toe beyond the boundaries of the business.

Mariano, Fulfillment Director. Mariano is the strong, silent type, who usually gets his point across with few words. He actually detests meetings that last longer than 10 minutes because much of his work is about moving product from Point A to Point B, and if you're in meetings, you're standing still. He is related to Ralph—Ralph's son is married to Mariano's sister, but that doesn't stop Ralph from chewing Mariano out on occasions when something falls through the cracks. Mariano leads by example and has a tendency to do the work himself before he delegates it to someone else.

Becky, Supply Chain Director. Becky at first appears to be this unassuming mild-mannered co-worker who is willing to help you in any way she can. But Becky always has an agenda. She grew up in the Guangzhou providence of China where we manufacture many of our products, and her experiences taught her to always be polite, even as she is hammering the final nail in your coffin. Her stubbornness has proven to be our asset, but it has gotten her into trouble as well. She is able to laugh or cry in meetings depending upon her objective and the outcome she wants to achieve.

Me, Operations Director. I wear 480 hats—that's one hat for every minute of a normal business day. My job is to implement ideas and clean up the mess when ideas don't work. My biggest frustrations come when we all don't get along (aren't we all on the same team? Don't we all have the same goals in mind?). My problem is that I don't take things too seriously. I take my job seriously, but I don't take people too seriously, especially anyone who thinks that the company can't go on without them. What gets me into trouble is when I have difficulty keeping a straight face. I also have low tolerance for lazy people who love to point out problems without offering solutions, and I find myself playing peacemaker more often than I should.

How in the world would I even get Jeff hired through this mixed bag of Directors? Should I tell them that I already have a hire and that we are just going through the motion? Naw... Marshall and Gail would break their necks to tell Ralph that I was circumventing his process and Becky would expect a hefty quid pro quo. Only Mariano would be on board with the streamlined process.

If this Hiring Committee was going to be our future, I had to play ball and take note of every step in the process. Dealing with these personalities all at once wasn't going to be fun. There would be times that I'd rather go through hell with gasoline underwear on. However, I knew that the challenging times like these would give me another great learning experience. Therefore, I decided to move ahead with the attitude that I would be the consummate student of the game.

| **The Hiring Committee**

Secret #1: Why Companies Hire

Why do companies hire in the first place? You may think that they hire because they want to fill a position, or because they are great places to work, or because they want you to join their team to achieve a goal.

That's what companies may sell, but the real reason why all companies across the board hire is because they are in pain. Yes, PAIN: **Profits Are In Need.**

That's it. It doesn't matter if it is a for-profit company, or a non-profit company, or a government agency, the reality is that companies don't want to hire you, they really don't. They would rather keep those dollars in their pocket than spend them on you because you are a huge expense. But when the pain of needing you outweighs the discomfort of not having you around, companies hire.

The #1 cause of company pain is customer service. When a company cannot meet the demands of its customers at its current capacity, it must hire to satisfy customer demand or risk losing profits.

This is why stores hire more people on weekends and after work hours, or why call centers are staffed more during peak hours, or why community health clinics recruit more practitioners—all so that customer's needs can be met and profits do not suffer.

The #2 cause of company pain is rising fixed costs such as rent, utilities, and yes, even health care costs. When these costs increase, companies must find ways to cover them, usually by decreasing other variable expenses or by increasing profits. In order to increase profits, companies will look to hire you.

Companies may never tell you they are in pain. They may say that they need someone, but in the recruiting process they never use the term pain to describe their need. They don't do that because they don't want to scare off candidates.

So the bottom line is that because companies are in business to stay in business, they will look to hire you when they are in pain.

Strategy #1: Assume the Customer Service role

What does all this mean for you? Now that you know their secret, you can use it to your advantage. Now that you understand that the company you are applying to is in pain, your job is to be their pain relief, primarily in the role of Customer Service.

What do you mean by the role of Customer Service?

This means that whatever job you are applying for, you want to communicate to the Hiring Committee (even if it is a committee of one) that you understand and acknowledge that your role is to provide great customer service. Yes, that's right. Since customer service is the pain producer for every business, when you sell yourself as a great customer service representative to any company throughout the hiring process, you stand out above the rest.

For example, if you are a receptionist, great customer service is engaging with people so that you start the customer's experience with the company off right. If you are in the tech industry, it is helping to produce products and services that customers would want to buy and share with others who will become customers themselves. If you are working in a warehouse, it is communicating with logistics to make sure that merchandise is available to customers.

To emphasize the last point, consider Kevin's story. Kevin was a warehouse worker who would bug the warehouse manager about getting products shipped to the stores as soon as they got in so that they would be available to the customer as soon as possible. When he was interviewing for another job, I told him to share this story with the Hiring Committee. He did, and they loved his customer service role even though his title was Warehouse Assistant.

In another example of great customer service, Don took a $5 per hour job working as a Sales Representative for Duty Free Shoppers (DFS) in the Los Angeles Airport. Yes, this was a long time ago. Don took the job after he had to file bankruptcy for his two restaurants that were closed due to non-payment of payroll taxes.

While at the store, an older gentleman came in to make a watch purchase. Don talked to him about the watch but the man seemed to have some reservations about the price. Don asked the man why he wanted the watch and he said that he wanted to give it to his father, who had a similar one but lost it during a relocation.

Don decided to use his own once-monthly employee discount option so that the man could buy the watch. The man thanked Don, bought it, and left the store. Two weeks later, Don was called to the corporate office. In the Senior VP's office was the man that Don sold the watch to. The Senior VP was impressed with Don's customer service, and in looking at Don's resume asked him why he took a job as a Sales Rep. Don said that he did so because he was in transition and wanted to keep busy while deciding his next career move.

The Senior VP offered Don a Regional Director's position which Don accepted. Don worked at DFS for over 20 years, eventually being promoted to Vice President of the northern region and successfully becoming one the top producing VPs in the company.

On the flip side, an example of terrible customer service was when I was flying to Missoula, Montana for a business trip. I parked my car at a nameless airport parking service called South Airport Parking. (Wait a minute, I thought I wasn't going to name them.)

When I pulled up, no one was at the lot. I honked once, waited 30 seconds and then honked again. This young girl came out wearing a tight, black tee shirt with bold yellow letters which said, "NOBODY ASKED YOU!"

The first thing out of her mouth was, "You didn't have to keep honking, I heard you the first time." I wanted to match her tee shirt attitude and say, *Did anybody ask you if I was honking for you? Maybe I just like honking…* But I was pinched for time. Needless to say, I haven't been back to South Airport Parking again. I predict that pretty soon their company will be in *P-A-I-N*.

So whatever job you are going through the hiring process for, make sure that you tout examples of your role in customer service. The Hiring Committee will love you for helping them ease their pain.

The story continues…

The process began with me having to inform the other directors of their selection (or requirement) to participate on the Hiring Committee. I could have sent out a group email, but because we had not hired a person quite this way before, I wanted to see each member's reaction. I started first in the office of the path of least resistance.

"Mr. Mariano, how are you doing, sir?"

"I'm doing well, Mr. Ed." I think that he called me this in reference to the 1960's TV Show, *Mr. Ed*, about a talking horse. That was the height of his humor.

"I just wanted to let you know that Ralph wanted you to be a part of the Hiring Committee for a Project Manager we need for ecommerce. We need your input to make sure that the person we hire knows that what they do for ecommerce affects what you need to do for fulfillment."

"Okay, so, what do you need for me to do?" Mariano asked.

"We just have to interview a couple of people and make a selection. We may have someone in mind already, but Ralph wants some input into the selection process. What I will do is find out what your best days are to meet and we'll get-in-get-out, knock-it-out-the-box, do all that and a bag of chips; bada-bing-bada-boom, that's it, we're done. Okay?"

"All right," Mariano said. I left and he went back to work.

I knew that Mariano would be easy if he felt that the Hiring Committee was going to be a short process. The fact that I made my request short was an indication to him that the whole process would be short as well. If I dragged on my request, he would stall and talk about all that he had to do and would short-change the process by probably selecting a candidate quickly even before seeing Jeff. Okay Mariano is in, now I went into Becky's office.

"Hi Becky!"

"Hello Eddie!" She said in her usual perky voice. I actually like Becky, even though she has a knack for trying to use her sweet little kind self to move her agenda along, even if it is pushing a square peg into a round hole.

I remember a time in dealing with Becky before when we had to pay a China shipping company we used to move merchandise from China to our warehouse. Becky sent me an email asking me to release the funds to the vendor. I was waiting on a report to verify the status of the email when Becky came to my office to have me try some Chinese cookies. I ate one politely, but found that they didn't have as much sugar and artificial sweeteners which I'm so accustomed to in my American cookies.

I thanked her for the cookie and told her that I needed to finish a document. She then took out another cookie and put it on a paper towel for me. As she did that, she asked me to do her a favor and send the payment to the vendor right away. She said that the vendor is asking her about the payment and wanted to have a favorable response to them.

I chuckled to myself, really wanting to be annoyed, but stopped what I was doing and did it anyway. She suckered me in with a Chinese cookie. What bothered me was something that Joel Olsten said: *The problem isn't that every man has a price, the problem is that their price is so low.*

With Becky in front of me now, I had to let her know about per participation on the Hiring Committee. I knew that it wasn't going to be as simple as telling her about it, and I knew that she was going to figure out how to leverage her role to her benefit.

"Becky, Ralph has assigned you to be a part of the Hiring Committee we are putting together for my Project Manager. I'll give you more details about it later, okay?"

"Hmm, Eddie, may I have some questions please?" (Oh boy, here we go!) "Why is Ralph doing this committee to hire your person? This is not normal."

I couldn't tell Becky that I didn't know why Ralph was doing this because that would give her more leverage for things she wanted me to do for her down the line. I had to be definitive in my response. "For two reasons: 1) He wants some formal input because the ecommerce project is going to affect all departments; and, 2) Because he said so." I said this with a hint of a smile so the message would come across like good medicine.

"Oh…," Becky said as her eyes looked heavenward as if she was pulling playing cards from the clouds in order to stack the deck. "Is Ralph going to do this for everyone now?"

"He might. It depends on the outcome of this Hiring Committee."

"What outcome is he looking for?" Becky asked.

Dammit! I just gave her fuel for the fire. I had to nip this in the bud. "Well, that remains to be seen, but I will give you an update soon, okay got to go..." I said walking out of her office. Whew! She almost sucked me in again for another item on her agenda.

I left and went to Gail's office. She has a tendency to talk a lot about people's personal lives and can be messy when talking about company business. I remember once she asked me if Lindsay, our bookkeeper, smoked marijuana on her lunch breaks because she was certain she smelled some "hay" on Lindsay one day as she returned from lunch.

Hay? What's that? Gail proceeded to run it down for me — pot, week, grass, herb, joint, Mary Jane, buds, Boo, broccoli, dank, ganja, 420 — how she knew all those terms made me think that she was the pot calling the kettle black (pun intended). I told Gail that I didn't get into anybody's personal business because I didn't want anybody in mine. I am very selective in what I say to Gail.

"Knock, knock!" I said as I knocked on Gail's door entering into her office. "Can I have 30 seconds of your time?"

"You can have more than that if you like, I'm just sitting here going over my emails," Gail said. She had a really pleasant voice and when she usually got back from vacation she would give me a hug and tell me how nice it was to see me. During those moments she reminded me of an older sister who could take care of things if mommy wasn't around.

I liked Gail in spurts. She had a knack for connecting with people which made her ideal for her job. Even though I wanted to get right to the point about the committee, I knew that whatever I said, I wasn't going to be able to drop it on her and leave. I had to give her some type of connection. "Wait a minute, something's different about your office since last week. Okay Gail, what did you change?"

"Oh Edwin, you noticed that I made a change. I moved these plants around so I could put up the photo of my grandson. He graduated this year."

"I knew something was different. What is your grandson's name again?" For the next several minutes Gail told me more than I ever cared to hear about her family. But I listened with great interest and let her speak before I got to the heart of the matter.

"You see, now you're going to make me forget why I stopped by to see you in the first place. Ralph is having me put a Hiring Committee together for the ecommerce project and you are on the committee. I should have everything together in a day or two and will give you everything you need."

"A Hiring Committee, huh? Who's all on the committee?" Gail asked as her face turned from Christmas to Halloween.

"All the Directors," I said. "Me, you, Marshall, Becky, and Mariano."

"Well this is new," she said. "And you're heading up the committee?"

"Yea, Ralph wants me to."

"Do you already have somebody in mind you're going to hire?" Gail asked. Boy, she was sharp. Gail was really sharp.

"I was thinking about hiring my grandmother," I said as we both laughed. I wasn't sure if I deflected Gail's suspicions enough, but I wasn't expecting her to be that sharp that quickly. "I'm not sure; I just think that Ralph wants more eyes on the project since this is new territory for us. Once I put something together, I'll get it to you, in about a day or so. Thanks Gail, nice plants." I knocked on her door twice again as I was leaving.

"Come back any time," I heard Gail say as I stepped out of her office. I waved as I kept on going.

Marshall. The Chief of Staff touted himself as the company's savior and boasted that he personally saved the company money more than anyone else. With his inability to be an effective communicator and lack of people-skills, Marshall has singlehandedly collected a record number of resignations from good employees.

He sends out emails in 6-point font to save the company paper; he gives Ralph a weekly report on who has come in late, left early, or taken an extended break; and, he makes his assistant keep nine cameras around her cubicle so he can monitor activity outside his office. (If you think I'm joking, see the actual photo below. Count the cameras.)

The balding 5-foot-1 overlord is a passive-aggressive Genghis Khan. He won't confront you to your face; instead, he will feed Ralph your head on a platter. He once informed Ralph of a manager who left early to meet his girlfriend at Starbucks and said to watch the manager's expense report to make sure there weren't any Starbucks receipts for that day.

As I headed towards Marshall's lair, I suddenly had a bout of indigestion. If it was gas, then my plan would be to release a silent bomb in Marshall's office upon my exit so he could feel *my* wrath for a change.

"Hey Marshall," I said walking through his door. I quickly looked around to make sure there were no guillotines with my name on them. "Did you hear that

Ralph put together a Hiring Committee for our ecommerce project?"

"Yes, Ralph mentioned it to me," Marshall said and he sat back in this chair interlocking his fingers under his chin with his two index finders pointing up in the air.

That bastard! How could he know if Ralph just told me 20 minutes ago before leaving for the day? Marshall must have orchestrated this whole Hiring Committee. That bastard! Now I'm really going to fart in his office when I leave.

"Oh, so he must have also mentioned that I'm chairing the committee and that you are on it with the other Directors," I said preparing myself that he already knew.

"That's a good thing," he said not really answering the question. "This is a very important project so it's good that everybody is involved."

"Ok good. I'll have something for everybody in a day or two. Thanks Marshall."

"Thank you Ed-win," he said smirking behind his wire-rimmed glasses.

I knew it, I knew it was him. Nobody calls me Ed-win while smirking through his glasses. He probably called me Ed-*win* knowing that I was planning to break wind in his office as I was leaving. I didn't have the courage to pass gas in his office fearing that he would have collected it somehow and brought it to Ralph to show him that I was trying to poison him, thus getting me fired. So I just left.

Back at my office I thought how the whole ordeal was somewhat painful. I really don't like playing company politics but we all have to do it. I would not go through this if I really didn't need a Project Manager. Jeff is the perfect person for the job and with him on board we could really ramp up the ecommerce project. Without him, I probably would have no life. Yep, I needed Jeff and so I needed to go through this Hiring Committee process.

My next step was to go through HR to get the process officially started.

SECRET #2: DEVELOPING THE JOB ANNOUNCEMENT

What is the big secret about how the job announcement is developed? Most Hiring Committees don't want you to know that usually only one person develops the job announcement, and the other committee members hardly look at it until it's time to interview candidates. Most companies want to present themselves as a team, a united front, and during the hiring process they don't want to let on about company politics, or schisms, or any divisions because they are trying to get you to join their team. In fact, if more than one person writes the job announcement, that's a formula for major delays in the Hiring Committee process. Therefore, most job announcements are developed by a single person.

Why? Well, think about it. If I'm the manager and I need a specific person, then I am going to create a job announcement based upon my needs without much input from other managers. This person works for me, not them, so my input is most important.

The great thing about writing the job announcement for a job I have is that I get to (hopefully) interview the candidates that fit my need. The not-so-good thing about this is that during the selection process I have to deal with feedback from those who don't have a stake in my department. During the interview we are supposed to act like a united front, but quite often there are agendas in the committee that may cause a good candidate to slip through the company's hands.

You can tell which companies only have one person developing the job announcement if any of these occur:

- Spelling and grammatical errors.
- Overuse of the term "preferred," especially when asking for credentials.
- Vagueness in describing roles or duties. (For example: "You will be given instructions on what to do on a daily basis…" Yes, this is from an actual job posting.)
- Using slang or hip terminology in the job announcement if the job isn't for a hip-hop artist.
- If there is no reference to salary. If more than one person developed the job announcement, there would normally be a reference to a salary.
- The minimum qualifications are so specific that only two people in the world could qualify for the job, and you're not one of them.

These are blatant indicators that the job announcement was solo-written. Many other job announcements are also written by one person, but then they may be reviewed by HR or another manager before being posted, so they may not have the missteps seen above. Whatever the case, there is a strategy in dealing with the job announcement.

Strategy #2: Address every area of the job announcement

Your strategy in dealing with each job announcement is to address every area of the job announcement. Why? Because that is how you score big points with any Hiring Committee, especially one where the job announcement was solo-written and the committee members are simply comparing your submission with the announcement.

In my book, _From Resume to Work,_ I detail the process on how you cover every area of the job announcement. This process includes:

1. Identify the qualifications on the job announcement.
2. List the qualifications in the order they appear.
3. After each qualification write one sentence on why or how you meet that qualification.
4. Remove the employer's qualification request leaving your list on how you cover every qualification.
5. Identify the responsibilities on the job announcement by reviewing the entire job announcement looking for any reference to what you might be doing or what you might be responsible for at the company.
6. Make a check list of all the responsibilities that you find (you can list them as bullet points initially as you did with the qualifications).
7. After each responsibility give an example on how you have handled a responsibility similar to what the employer wants you to do.
8. Remove the employer's responsibilities leaving your own list giving examples of how you can do that responsibility.

Following these steps will not only help your submission get to the Hiring Committee, but will also help you through the Hiring Committee process because you are showing the committee, as well as the solo job announcement writer, that you are the best candidate for the job.

The story continues...

Although I was solely in charge of writing the job description, I was determined to avoid the vague, horribly misspelled listings I'd seen in the past. I also needed to make sure the description was tailored to my perfect candidate. That way, HR would immediately notice him and send him to the committee, and I could get on with convincing the other Directors that we needed this perfect candidate, who of course is Jeff.

HR has a standard blurb about the company that goes at the beginning of every job listing, so I started with the actual description of the job:

The Project Manager is responsible for rolling out the company's ecommerce project from start to finish while remaining on budget. This role is crucial in developing the company's ecommerce business and managing the day-to-day details. The Project Manager will integrate the departments, provide training and support, and ensure important tasks get completed in a timely manner. The position reports to the Operations Director.

Because blocks of text in job descriptions often just get skimmed, I also listed out the specific details in bullet points:

- *Manages the project from beginning to completion*

- *Works with various departments to ensure the project transitions seamlessly from one stage into the next*

- *Assigns tasks to department representatives and follows up regularly with the representatives to confirm all duties are being carried out as specified*

- *Creates and maintains a reasonable budget and strives to stay within the limits of that budget*

- *Ensures the project is completed within the assigned timeframe and meets or exceeds management expectations*

- *Willing to go above and beyond in order to reach the project's goals*

- *Promotes company standards throughout the life of the project*

From there, I moved to the qualifications for the job. I wanted these to line up with Jeff's resume so there could be no doubt that he was not only capable, but seemingly created just for this job. I opened his resume and read it over. Jeff started his career as a computer programmer, working on online banking websites before he moved on to develop several ecommerce systems for different banks. His most recent projects were with a company that created an online payment system based on PayPal. He had a B.S. in computer science and an MBA.

Based on Jeff's info, I made a list of qualifications that included:

- *Successful management and completion of vital company projects*

- *Proven problem-solving skills*

- *Ability to communicate effectively with employees at all levels*

- *Consistent metrics delivery on a weekly basis*

- *Effective delegation of responsibilities and following up on these tasks*

- *Ability to provide a clear and specific outline/plan for each project, including objectives, goals, costs, tasks, and all other pertinent information*

- *Excellent chart making abilities*

- *Expert-level Excel capabilities*

- *Technological savvy: ability to train other employees to use the new systems needed for project implementation*

- *Ten years' experience with ecommerce positions within financial institutions*

- *Bachelor's degree (required), MBA (preferred)*

Reading over the list, I felt pretty good about myself. Perhaps I should do this HR thing for a living and relieve Connie of her HR duties. Yea, that wouldn't work. Ralph wouldn't pay me any more money.

The job description encompassed what I personally looked for in a project manager, plus it included a little something extra that I knew Jeff could bring to the table and that few others might be able to match.

I printed out my description and took it to Connie's office. Connie is the head of HR. Anything up for posting goes through her for approval. We have a great relationship but she often irks me. "Hi Connie!" I said. "I've got a little something here for you." I held up my paper.

Connie smiled and waved me in. "Hello, sir," she said. "Is this for the project manager role?"

"Yes ma'am." I handed her the paper and sat down at the chair across from her desk. "I was hoping you could give it a quick glance, if you're not too busy. I'm on a tight timeline so I wanted to get it posted ASAP." I flashed my most charming smile in the hopes that I could get her to comply.

"No problem," she said. "I understand."

"You, Connie, are my favorite." I pressed my hand to my heart dramatically.

She smiled and put on her glasses. Her eyes narrowed as she looked over what I'd written. "Ten years?" she asked, glancing up at me.

I'll admit, the ten years' experience was probably overboard. But I wanted to scare off a lot of people.

I shrugged. "Not good?"

"Well…" She sat back and took off her glasses. "Overall, this is pretty good. But some of your qualifications are a little too… on the nose. Too specific," she clarified. "We need the job description to appeal to a fairly wide mass of project managers. Otherwise, the hiring process will drag on forever."

Oops. I might have aligned my job description a little *too* closely to Jeff's experience. "You see Connie, this is why they pay you the big bucks," I said. She smiled and rolled her eyes.

"Okay," I said. "So what do I need to change?"

She took out a red pen and began marking on the paper as she spoke. "Well, first off, I don't think a master's degree is necessary for this position, right?"

"You're probably right," I agreed.

"So we don't even need to mention it. Also, you should reduce the years of experience and make it more general," she said. "Like, for experience, don't put things like 'experience working on projects in such-and-such field.' Instead, say, 'Five years' experience leading company projects with increasing responsibility,' and 'a minimum of three years' experience in ecommerce.'"

"Why five and three years?" I asked. "Just curious."

She shrugged. "So you don't wind up interviewing a bunch of newbies who did one mock ecommerce project at business school and think that makes them a bona fide professional," she said. "Five years is long enough that a person should be pretty qualified, but not so long that they ask for the sun and moon during pay negotiations."

"Ah, I see," I said, knowing full well I'd be quite open to whatever Jeff suggested when it came to compensation. A good project manager is worth every penny. "Any other changes?"

Once again, her red pen flew over the paper. "Just include the stock info. You know, like, office job, salary position, overtime exempt, and if it includes a certain percentage of travel. Put the normal office hours, but if you think this job will extend beyond the usual 9-to-5, be sure to include that. People get bent out of shape when they're thrown a curveball, especially if that curveball is unpaid overtime." She smiled at me.

I smiled back, relieved that she didn't muck up my work too much. "Gotcha," I said. "I'll be sure to let them know we keep a cot in the basement and they're allowed a fifteen-minute nap every night before they go back to doing my bidding all day."

Her smile widened. "Now you've got it!"

I tapped my temple. "Not just a hat rack, my friend," I said. She laughed.

"Here you go," she pushed the paper back to me. "I added in our boilerplate HR stuff. I've read it so much over the years that I have it memorized." She rolled her eyes. "I'm not sure if that's a talent or just plain sad."

"Connie, you are anything but sad," I replied.

"Gee, thanks."

"No, thank you," I said. "Seriously. Thanks for helping me get this done and out the door so fast." I gathered my redlined document and headed back to my office. I implemented Connie's changes, then checked and double-checked my work. The last thing I needed was for HR to come after me. The moment I was satisfied, I posted the job on Indeed.com, then sent it to HR to post on our Careers page.

Secret #3: Processing Submissions

For small businesses, usually the person writing the job announcement is the same person who receives the resume submissions, but that is not always the case. In larger companies resume submissions go through HR and then they are funneled to the hiring manager or the point person on the Hiring Committee.

What happens far too often is that your resume falls through the cracks and is lost to follow up. That may be why you haven't heard back from anyone; not because you had a substandard resume, but because somebody is not doing their job and handling your resume as it should be handled.

Companies don't want you to know this.

They don't want you to know that they have cracks in their organization. My wife told me a story where she wanted to hire a nurse for one of her clinics. Two weeks after the job was posted she hadn't received a single resume from HR. When she contacted HR, she was told she hadn't received any responses. After two more weeks and no responses, she called HR again and was told there were still no responses. My wife received a letter from an applicant asking if the position was still available since it was still posted but she had received no response to her submission.

My wife sent a copy of the letter to her boss asking her to have a conversation with HR. Three days later my wife received 27 responses to the posting. Apparently, somebody in HR let stuff fall through the cracks—it probably was the person they fired a month later.

Strategy #3: Submit your resume twice

Yes, submit your resume a second time. You do this for several reasons: (1) Just in case your initial resume fell through the cracks; (2) To get a second chance to make a first impression; and, (3) To show your potential employer that you have great follow-up skills.

When you send your initial resume (and cover letter), make sure that you follow the submission process in the exact way they say. If they tell you not to resubmit your application, then do not send your resume again.

How long should you wait before sending your resume again? It has been my experience with those employers I talked with about receiving a follow-up submission, and the consensus is usually 2-3 weeks after you have submitted it or after you have received notice that your resume was received. This is true even if resume submissions had a closing date, you can still resend your resume and cover letter referring to the resume that you submitted before the closing date.

What should you say when you resend your resume? When you submit your resume, you definitely want to include a separate cover letter. If the submission process doesn't allow you to submit a separate cover letter, then create a two-page resume in which the first page is the cover letter (that is if your resume is one page). The point is that you want to explain why you are sending your resume again.

In your second submission cover letter here are some points to cover or say:

- Look at your cover letter that you initially sent with your first resume. Do not send the same cover letter. You want your follow-up cover letter to sound like an actual follow-up letter.

- Here is an example of how you could begin your follow-up letter: *Dear Hiring Committee, I previously submitted my resume on (date) and I am just following up with you on your job announcement. I am including another copy of my resume...*

- *I am really excited about working for your company because...* (No not just because you want the job or that you are currently unemployed. Say something that reflects that you feel like you are perfect for the job.)

- *In your job announcement you stated that you are looking for* (state something from the job announcement), *and as you can see on my resume I have* (show them that you meet the qualification of that specific area they are looking for) ...

- Make sure that you specifically reference duties and qualifications from their job announcement. The most powerful cover letters cover every point on the job announcement. For more details about how to cover every point on your cover letter, please see *From Resume to Work*.

- Intentionally add a postscript (P.S.) at the end of this cover letter, saying something like: *You can call me at* (number) *or email me at* (email) *to get in touch with me right away. I am looking forward to your call.*

I do not recommend sending a third resume. That's because at that point you will be perceived as annoying (unless you're applying for a high-pressure sales job), and that would more than likely get you booted from the submission process. However, by sending a follow-up resume, you can increase your chances of standing out above the crowd.

The story continues...

Resumes started piling in. They all went to HR initially, who shuffled through them and removed candidates that failed to meet the most basic requirements of the job before sending me the rest. I spent each morning going through the batch from the previous day, sending some to my own "Immediate Elimination" pile and hanging onto the few I saw who might be good for the "Telephone Interview" pile.

I came home from work the night the job was posted on the company's site and called Jeff to advise him to skip applying on Indeed and go straight to our website to apply. Generally, resumes coming to HR's email address got viewed a little quicker than the ones coming from employment websites. My goal was to get his resume into the right hands as quickly as possible.

My plan appeared to work because Jeff's was one of the first resumes HR sent over. I looked it over briefly to make sure he made at least most of the changes we had discussed. It looked pretty darn perfect. I added him to the top of my telephone interview pile.

The next step was to find a handful of other candidates that looked good, maybe even very good, but when they were put up against Jeff, they would fall short. Obviously, I couldn't pick a bunch of unqualified people and Jeff – I'd look incompetent and the committee would immediately know something was up.

My resume selection process has been perfected over the years – at least, in my humble opinion. I have hired many employees and reviewed even more resumes, so I would like to think I knew a thing or two about how to find the right person for a job.

First things first, my "Immediate Elimination" pile. Like I said, HR took care of many duds so they never actually reached me. But there was only so much HR knew to look for, so there would always be at least a few, and maybe as much as half the stack, that would immediately get the ax.

Here are reasons why I would chuck your resume right away:

- **Spelling errors**. If you have a spelling error, you should expect a rejection. In fact, if you have grammar mistakes or misspellings, and a company still calls you? You should seriously consider declining their offer for an interview. I mean, do you really want to work for a company that hires sloppy employees who can't even correctly spell all the words on their resume?

- **You've had a million jobs in the past few years**. Project managers might be involved in a lot of different projects, but unless they're consultants that work for themselves, I'm not too interested in the candidates who spend only a few months at a job before moving on. You may be excellent at your job, but I just can't imagine any project taking so little time. At least, the ones I've worked on sure haven't.

- **You haven't worked anywhere in the past few years**. I'm not talking a few jobless months or even a year. I understand it can be difficult to find a job sometimes. But if you've been actively searching for five years and you haven't filled that time with freelance work or even an unpaid mentorship or internship, I'm going to worry that you're either not as experienced as you claim, or maybe you're not as determined to find work as you want me to believe. Plus, being out of the loop five years could put you very behind, technologically speaking, and I don't want to spend months getting you up-to-date on the latest computer programs, or even Microsoft Office. (Heaven help you if you don't know Microsoft Office.)

- **There's too much fluff and not enough substance**. All I can determine from these resumes is that you have an intense relationship with your thesaurus. Don't try to reimagine newer, fancier ways to say "I organized weekly meetings with the executive team." Just tell it to me straight – I want to know what you did, what you know, and what you can bring to my team.

- **Your social media accounts paint a different picture of you**. This may seem unfair because it's your personal Facebook or Twitter account, and not your professional resume. But be warned: companies do check you out online. If you have a bunch of inappropriate pictures or posts, I may wonder if I'm getting to see the "real" you. And I may not like what I see.

These rules are not all-inclusive, and I have been known to occasionally break them, bad boy that I am. But they're a pretty good set to keep in mind when you're getting your resume ready for a job. Heck, maybe I should write a book about this stuff. Oh, wait! I already did. It's called *From Resume to Work*. It's a good read if you're looking to get the full extent of my experience and advice.

Now that I've spent all this time being negative and nitpicky, you may be wondering if I find any resumes impressive. The short answer is yes. There are definitely good applicants surrounded by a pile of not-so-good ones, which is why we have this double-review process. A lot of the characteristics I like to see are the converse of the ones I don't like. For example:

- **You can show me the money**. I want to see what you've accomplished for your past companies. Did you save them money? Did you make them money? Are you single-handedly responsible for some amazing, life-changing process or system that brought your company back from the brink of extinction (or, at the very least, made everyone's lives a bit easier)? I want you to tell me about it and spare no details.

- **You have some loyalty**. Now, I don't expect everyone to have a resume showing they've been with a company for decades. That's not realistic, especially in the modern world, where people no longer spend their entire working lives at one job and retire with a gold watch. But I'd like to see that you gave each of your employers at least one year, and preferably a bit more time. This shows me you spent enough time with them to learn the ins and outs and give your job a chance. It also means they actually know who you are and what you did if I decide to call them for a reference.

- **You look good on paper and online**. If you have an impressive resume and your social media accounts don't raise red flags, I'm definitely going to want to interview you.

- **You work well with others**. We already have one Marshall, and I'm not looking to duplicate him. It's important that you get along with your co-workers in any role, but for a project manager, it's crucial. Project managers hold many meetings and need to be able to communicate well with employees at all levels. They also have to assign tasks to others and make sure those people are doing what they need to do. Otherwise, the whole project can get off track or fail. If that happens, who do you think takes the blame?

While shifting through my pile of resumes, I found some comparable candidates to put up against Jeff in the interviewing process. I selected five candidates: Robert, Paula, Kathy, Jamila, and Daniel. All of them had good backgrounds and seemed quite capable. But I didn't think they looked nearly as strong as Jeff, and I was confident when all was said and done, the committee would agree with me.

I made a zip file of all six resumes and emailed to the other committee members, asking if they had time to sit in on telephone screens for them. Phone screens were short and annoying, but they could help us whittle down our list. If I could get everyone on board with the phone screens, we could knock these all out in a day or two and actually start bringing some people into the office.

I marked the email as "Important" and requested a read receipt. After the last email debacle, I decided I need to keep track of everyone. By the end of the day, I knew that all of them had at least opened the email, so the next morning, I sent a follow-up about phone screens.

Marshall responded that he was tied up in meetings for the rest of the week and wouldn't have time to screen candidates. Mariano, the king of brevity, simply forwarded Marshall's response and wrote "Same." Becky said she would be out of town, but Gail agreed to help. I asked her to contact Paula, Kathy, and Jamila, while I tackled Jeff, Robert, and Daniel. So the fun begins.

Secret #4: Telephone Interviews

What's the big secret about telephone interviews? For one thing, many companies don't do them, and for those that do, they are usually not handled by the decision-maker for the position because telephone interviews lack body language, visual prompts, and chemistry. Most interviewers prefer looking at how someone responds instead of just hearing how they respond.

Companies who do phone interviews don't want to let you know that the phone call is quite often a formality because they have already decided to bring you in for a face-to-face interview, but just want to check the "We talked to them ahead of time" box for the HR process.

Unless you do something crazy, like flush the toilet during your phone interview or have "We're not going to take it?" blasting in the background, you could be pretty confident that they want to bring you in if you follow the script.

Strategy #4: Follow the script

What does follow the script mean? During a phone interview, the interviewer has a script that they are following, and they expect you to follow along. Their script is your resume or CV that they have in front of them. They will ask you a series of questions and are looking for answers that you have already provided them on your resume. It is your job to provide them with answers that are consistent to what is on your resume.

In one telephone call, I made a mistake and called one person but somehow had another person's Page 2 of their resume. When I asked about their ability to use Goal Seek in Excel that was on their resume, they muddle up an unacceptable answer. When I realized I had the wrong resume Page 2, I saw that they didn't have Goal Seek Excel skills, which wasn't required, but then realized that this person lied or didn't know their resume. It would have been better for them to say, "I don't have Goal Seek Excel on my resume. You must have called me because I have other exceptional skills." That's following the script.

Therefore, your strategy before taking the call is to reread your entire resume at least twice, and then have your resume in front of you as you are on the phone. You don't have to look at your resume when you're answering the question. In fact, for some people it is best to stand up and move around while you're talking because that helps put enthusiasm in your voice as you're speaking. (I wouldn't recommend doing something extraneous because you might get winded while you're on the phone which would be a distraction to the interviewer.)

However, your script not only includes your resume, but it also includes the job announcement as well.

Never attempt to handle a phone interview without your resume *and* the job announcement. That is why you should always keep a copy of every posting that you respond to and make it easily accessible.

I would often tell job information participants that they should print out and keep the posting in a hard copy file, or scan it and keep it in a file on their computer, or email it to themselves, or better yet, store it in a cloud folder.

Before the interview, always review the minimum qualifications but pay close attention to the duties and responsibilities section of the announcement. You most likely already meet the minimum qualifications or you would not have received the call. So focus on the duties and responsibilities and keep them in front of you as you listen to the questions.

When you give your answers, make sure you follow the script and give answer consistent with your resume but that also satisfy a duty or responsibility on the job announcement.

The story continues...

Like I said before, the phone screen is the first of the two-part interviewing process. Phone interviews consist of a handful of stock questions that help us confirm our candidate understands our company, what we do, and what is expected of them. It also helps establish salary, so we don't bring in someone expecting $150,000 when we're prepared to offer $85,000.

I sent Gail the Interview Questionnaire checklist I got from HR. It has our questions and space to write any comments. The questions we use are:

- Tell me about your current role.

- Why are you leaving your current company?

- Why do you think you'd be good for this role?

- What is your expected salary?

- Are you willing to travel?

- Are you okay with working nights and weekends, if necessary?

- Describe a successful project/idea/etc. that you spearheaded.

- Describe a particularly challenging situation you faced, and what you did to overcome it.

- What are your strengths?

- What are your weaknesses?

- Do you have any questions for me?

Now, I will be the first to admit that I am not the biggest fan of some of these questions. I particularly loathe the "strengths and weaknesses" questions because I've heard the pat answers: "I'm probably too organized," or "Some would say I have almost too much dedication to my job," so many times. But I get it.

The question was designed, as were many of the others, to see how people think on their feet. I don't put much weight into a person's answer to these questions, although I have gotten a few responses to it that actually appeared sincere. Before launching into the questions, we give a basic overview of the company as well as the position. HR provided their stock company overview on the Questionnaire, and I included a few sentences about the job itself, sort of like a refresher for the interviewee.

True to my word, I called Robert and Daniel and went through the Interview Questionnaire, word for word. I might not be interested in hiring them, but I was willing to give them a chance. Just as their resumes suggested, they were both competent employees that some company will be lucky to have. Robert, for example, described in great detail a particularly complex project he had managed and was able to get completed within his designated timeframe and on budget. It was actually quite impressive.

I told him it was no small feat to pull that off on his first project, especially one as involved as his. But the problem was, that was about all he had done. And Jeff had done projects just like the one Robert described, but he did more and could give solid figures indicating how much money he had saved past companies.

Daniel had some great management experience. He told me he was very organized and excellent at assigning duties to his employees and holding them accountable.

He said that even though these tasks must be completed by others, he was ultimately responsible, so he made sure to keep everyone on track. He was great at speaking, so he would likely do well communicating with the department heads, which was vital to this role. And he had worked on some projects, but he couldn't point to a lot of cases where he was the sole manager of any of them.

To be honest, they were both great. But they didn't blow me away. Jeff's experience and past employment far outweighed both Robert and Daniel put together.

I decided not to bother calling Jeff. I had been in touch with him enough to know all his answers, so I spent some time filling in his questionnaire by myself before heading to Gail's office to see how her phone screens went.

"Knock-knock!" I said, holding up my papers.

"Hi Edwin!" she smiled. "Come in."

I closed her door and sat down at the small table in her office. She got up from her desk and came over to join me. "How's your day going?" I asked. I was ever mindful of the fact that Gail likes chit-chat, so I didn't usually just jump into things with her.

"Very well, thanks," she said. "I found the perfect set of luggage to get my grandson for his graduation present."

"Oh yeah? That's a nice gift."

"Thanks." She smiled, satisfied. "I think they will serve him well when he's packing for college." She described a couple of his acceptance letters and his thoughts about attending an out-of-state choice over an in-state school.

As soon as I felt we had a decent lull in the conversation, I asked, "Ready to talk candidates?"

"Sure."

"I'm happy to report that I did have some luck," I said nonchalantly. "How about you?"

"I think so," she replied smugly, patting a small pile of paper on the table in front of her. "Let's hear about your guys first."

"Okay," I said. "Well, I interviewed the three men. Two of them, named…" I pretended to lean forward and study the names, as if I couldn't actually remember who they were. "Ah, yes, Robert and Daniel. To be honest, I was pretty 'meh' about both of them."

"Oh, really?"

"Yes. I mean, they're good. They have some great resumes. But their experience felt a little incomplete and isn't related to us or ecommerce. Plus, they just didn't have that 'wow factor' I was hoping to find."

"That can be difficult to come across," Gail said.

"Exactly!" I said. "I sometimes feel like I'm asking for too much when I look for it. But then I talked to Jeff." I held up my questionnaire for emphasis. "And *this* guy… He has it."

"Really?" Gail's eyes went wide. "That's amazing!" But I thought that she sounded a little off. Doubtful, perhaps?

"Yes! I was in a constant state of shock while we were speaking." I began ticking points off on my fingers. "I mean, he has experience that actually lies in our field. He's spearheaded a number of big projects and had great results, and his salary is definitely in our range. Oh, *and*, he has such a great personality. He didn't have one negative thing to say about anyone." I shook my head in mock amazement. "It's like he was created for this position."

"He certainly sounds like he was," Gail said. She was smiling, yet I still had a feeling I hadn't convinced her that I'd found our guy.

"Anyway, enough about the Amazing Jeff," I said. "You said you found someone, too?"

Gail's grin broadened. "I did," she said. "Two someone's, actually."

Uh oh.

"No kidding," I said, hoping my smile didn't seem as forced as it felt. "Two?"

"Yes," she said. "Jamila and Paula. I thought Kathy seemed very nice, but she just didn't have the experience that the other two had."

I leaned back a bit in my chair. "Okay," I said. "Let's have some details."

"Well, I talked to Jamila first. She's a Project Manager right now at her current company and she's done project work for past employers as well. Her experience seemed right in line with what we do," Gail said, pushing her resume over to me.

Of course, I wanted to object, but instead, I glanced at the resume and said, "Oh, right, I remember this one. She does seem to have a lot of experience," I said, with a slight emphasis on the word "seem." Gail didn't appear to notice.

"Then I talked to Paula. She's got some good experience, but perhaps even better, she's got a reference we can talk to."

"Who?" I demanded.

"Eban."

"Eban?" I was puzzled. "As in, Ralph's son?"

"Exactly," Gail purred. "Paula has worked with Eban on past projects. They put together these small business seminars. She had nothing but nice things to say about him," Gail added.

Well, of course, she did. Did Gail think this woman would trash the son of the CEO of our company when she wanted to work here? I pretended to peruse Paula's resume while I thought. The fact that Paula knew Eban could either be helpful or hurtful; I wasn't sure which one just yet.

"I wonder if it's such a good idea to involve Eban on this?" I said.

"What do you mean?"

"Well," I said, "I just don't know if we should ask Eban what he thinks of Paula just yet. It seems a little early. I mean, if you like her, maybe we should all talk to her first before talking to a reference. Even if that reference *is* Eban. Don't you think?"

"Sure, that makes sense," Gail said. "I do think we should have Paula come in for an interview with the committee. Afterwards, if we love her, we could ask Ralph to check with Eban."

"Sounds good," I said. "Okay, so it looks like we're passing on Robert, Daniel, and Kathy, and we want to submit Paula, Jamila, and Jeff for interviews. Would you agree?"

"Agreed."

"Okay, great. I'll let HR know and we'll get those set up. Also, can I have your interview notes? I'll send both sets of our notes out to the rest of the committee." I stood up and gave a mock bow. "Thank you so much for your help, kind lady," I said in a formal tone.

Gail tittered. "Oh, Edwin, you're such a character!" she said.

Back in my office, I emailed interview notes to the committee while I considered Paula's association with Eban. As I said, Eban is Ralph's son, but their relationship is a little strained. They don't talk much – in fact, it only seemed that Eban came around to visit his father when he wanted money.

When he was in college, Eban told his father that he didn't want to inherit Ralph's company and would rather make something for himself, doing something he actually wanted to do. It was an admirable thought, except Eban didn't seem to have the business sense (or the startup capital) to flesh out his ventures. He'd go to his parents, brimming with excitement over his newest plan, asking Ralph to become an investor. Ralph would say no every time, explaining to Eban that he could hardly be considered an investor when he never even made his money back on these businesses, much less a profit of any sort. He would point out potential pitfalls in the businesses or just tell him flat-out when he thought an idea was never going to work. Eban would sulk and claim his father never believed in him.

For the next week or so, Ralph's wife would needle him until he gave in and lent Eban the money. After a few months, the business would tank, and Ralph would be out whatever dollar amount he'd given his son. Then in another six months or a year, the vicious cycle would repeat again.

Because Ralph didn't think much of his son's business sense (or lack thereof, if we're being honest), he might not have much respect for anyone who would work with Eban. Maybe I should run Paula past Ralph and ask him if her association with Eban mattered or not. He might say it didn't matter, or he might even say anyone connected to Eban's questionable businesses could not possibly be considered for a position with us.

In either of those scenarios, I could potentially lift Paula right out before the interviews started, claiming that Paula's association with Eban wasn't impressive enough. But what if Ralph actually did care? Or, what if Paula's relationship with Eban actually put her in a more favorable light? Going to Ralph and mentioning Paula could be the wrong move because he might take an interest in her (or worse, ask to sit in on the interview).

In the end, I decided that Ralph didn't need to know about Paula and Eban. And no matter who she knew, Paula's resume wasn't as great as Jeff's. I firmly believed she simply wouldn't be able to stand up to him. I might have laid it on a bit thick in my meeting with Gail, but I wasn't kidding when I said Jeff was practically made for the job. It would be irresponsible and unprofessional of us to choose the candidate with connections over the candidate with actual qualifications. I just hoped the rest of the committee would see it that way, too.

Secret #5: Before the Interview

Although you may want to think that you're special because you were selected for a face-to-face interview, the reality is that you're just another candidate on this side of the interview, until you wow them and get on that side of the interview.

After companies select you for an interview, they don't spend much time thinking about you, what they should ask you, and why they are asking you — they go on with their own business lives. Many of them don't prep before the interview, and sadly some of them don't even see your resume until right before you walk in. That's the reality of it. The only person besides you who would be excited about your interview would be the person who you would directly report to.

You may think that the lack of preparation of some of your Hiring Committee members would make your job of convincing them that you are the best candidate for the position a lot harder, but on the contrary, the less prepared they are the better it is for you.

Why?

Because they would be following a script — basically looking at the job announcement, a list of interview questions, and your resume. If that's the script they are following, then your job just got easier. What you have to do is to look at yourself from a committee member's point of view. Then committee members who are following a script can check all the boxes that relate to the job announcement and your resume (i.e., are they qualified to do the job).

Strategy #5: Interview yourself before the interview

Although Hiring Committee members may not spend much time preparing for your interview, you must spend the time preparing for it.

I have conducted many mock interviews and they are definitely good practice to help you for interview. During my job information workshop days, I would use an actual job posting and then add an element of pressure to the mock interview where I would incentivize the participants who were interviewing, doing something like offering a $50 gift card to the one who "got the job."

I would also have participants act as Hiring Committee members where they interview candidates for the position and then rank which applicant they liked and why. Then I would turn it back around and have them interview for the same job again. All this would be done in an open setting where everyone could hear everyone else's interviews. And the rules were that they could use any response they heard during the mock sessions.

The second time around every participant made a marked improvement in their interview. One of the main reasons was because they got the opportunity to sit in the employer's seat and see what they wanted to hear from a candidate.

Therefore, you must prepare by interviewing yourself for the job you want. You can do this by taking the job announcement and your resume and then sitting down at a desk and asking "you" questions.

When you ask a question, you can respond by either thinking about what response you'd want to hear or actually responding out loud, perhaps in front of a mirror.

Listed below are interview questions you can use to practice interviewing yourself on. They don't have to be in any order necessarily.

- Tell me about yourself.
- Why do you want this job?
- Why did you leave your last job?
- What are your greatest strengths?
- What are your greatest weaknesses?
- How well do you work under pressure?
- Describe a difficult work situation and how you overcame it.
- What makes you uniquely qualified for this position?
- In this job you will be required to (state something from the duties and responsibilities section of the job announcement). Give me an example of how you have performed this task in the past.

- Tell me something about yourself that would make me not want to hire you for this job. (Forgive me for this question, as 99% of people I've asked this have failed to answer it acceptably. Unfortunately, a number of people have unwittingly shot themselves in the foot, giving up information like their drug use or sexual peculiarities. I now only use this question as a weapon when someone tries to shove a candidate down my throat. The best response I received to date was, "I am driven and sometimes bordering on being a workaholic. If you're trying to keep the status quo, then you may not want to hire me for this job." I hired them, and they turned out to be one of my best hires.)

You should interview yourself several times before the interview. You can never prepare for every question or every nuance the committee may throw at you, but at least you'll be better prepared than if you did little or nothing at all. Here are a list of 50 tough interview questions from Monster.com (/HIRING22).

The story continues...

Trying to schedule these interviews was proving to be about as fun as getting a tooth pulled without any Novocain. I couldn't even get my fellow committee members to spend a few minutes perusing a job description. Now I was expected to get them into a room for four hours to actually meet our candidates?

I started the interview-scheduling process in a mass email. In the body of my email, I informed everyone that I was trying to keep this whole thing as painless as possible, so I planned to schedule all three interviews back-to-back on the same day. Looking over everyone's online calendar doesn't always help, since they don't necessarily keep them current (or they are unable to employ admins to do that for them). But I did a quick peruse and put together a handful of days and times when everyone was free, so I added those suggestions to my email. I stressed the fact that we were on a short timeline and needed to get something on the calendar fairly quickly. Once again, I marked the email "Important" and checked the read receipt box so I would know who was bothering to read their email that day.

As expected, I got no response that day, but I was able to confirm that everyone but Becky opened their email. The next day I sent a follow-up, informing everyone that I hadn't heard back from them (duh) so I was going to choose the first day and time in my list of choices to schedule the interviews. This time, all four of them opened the email, and I finally got a response from Becky by lunchtime that day, letting me know she couldn't do the first or second time slots in my email but that she could make the third or fourth times. Mariano said he was free for the third time slot, but Gail could only do the fourth one, and Marshall finally replied at the end of the day, saying none of the dates and times worked for him. Crap.

The next two days were dedicated to finding a time to schedule interviews. I didn't know whether to laugh or cry. As I'd predicted from the beginning, the Hiring Committee was basically a big, time-sucking roadblock. I had my perfect candidate, only I couldn't even get him through the door because coordinating the schedules of these four suddenly-super-busy people was impossible. When I finally got a date scheduled, two weeks out, I considered sending the email chain to Ralph and asking for – no, *demanding* a raise. This might have been the most difficult task of my employment so far.

After locking down a day, it was time to call the candidates themselves and schedule times. I considered what order I wanted the interviews to move. Should I start with Jeff, while everyone was fresh and attentive? Or should I end with him, letting him make a great impression that stuck in everyone's minds, allowing them to completely forget anything about the other candidates? I wrote down my possible lineups:

Paula-Jamila-Jeff: Paula, who could possibly be my biggest threat due to her relationship with Ralph's son, would go first so that she could become a distant memory in the minds of the committee members. Putting Jeff at the end would hopefully make him the most memorable, especially since he is truly the best candidate.

Jeff-Paula-Jamila: Like I said, putting Jeff first would mean he was meeting the committee when they were at their freshest and most responsive. Plus, I could ask him lots of questions that would both show off his skills and cause us to run over our half-hour, leaving us less time to meet with the other candidates and therefore forcing us to cut their interviews short.

Jamila-Paula-Jeff: Another theory I thought about testing was that the middle candidate was the easiest to forget. Putting Paula here basically would turn her into a blip on the screen. In my opinion, Jamila was not nearly as strong as Jeff, so the committee would only remember how great he was and I'd finally get to put him on the team.

Jeff-Jamila-Paula: After much thought, this was the line-up I decided to use. I would ask Jeff a bunch of questions that showed off his expertise and thought process and I would make it my goal to put us over his time limit, making Paula's interview the shortest. By the time Paula got there, the committee would be hungry, tired, and antsy to go. They would probably ask a couple of standard questions and barely remember the answers.

But just before I had HR schedule the interviews, I changed my mind. Maybe the lineup should be Jeff-Paula-Jamila. I knew it was somewhat of a risky move to take Paula out of the third time slot, especially since it put her right next to Jeff. I worried that the committee might feel they need to pick her as a sign of loyalty to Ralph – they don't all know about his difficult relationship with Eban.

But ultimately, I thought having Jeff and Paula next to each other would provide an excellent contrast of what each of them could bring to the table. The committee members would see that Jeff is obviously more qualified, so the thought of hiring someone just because she did a couple of projects with the boss's son would seem ridiculous. And Jamila was clearly the weakest of the three, so keeping her last and cutting her interview short was not going to make a difference.

With my schedule set, I called Paula and Jamila and scheduled their times. On my way home, I called Jeff from my personal cell phone to confirm his time. I didn't call him at work because I didn't want to risk anyone overhearing my conversation with him. We went over the interview questions, and I briefly described the directors and gave him a few pointers on how to handle the committee. I wished him luck, but at this point, I didn't think he needed it.

Secret #6: Committee Member Dynamics

Hiring Committees don't want you to know that for the most part they all don't really like each other. You would probably never see them out to lunch together, unless it was a mandatory working lunch. And for many Hiring Committees that have three or more bodies, it wouldn't be difficult to feel at least some of the underlying tension between certain members.

Committee members may respect each other, they may respect the position and authority each has, but as a whole most of them have one thing or another against someone else.

Committee member dynamics often have unintended consequences for you, particularly, not getting the job you want and that you are qualified to do. Rest assured that the issues of a bad interview may not necessarily be a reflection upon you, but rather it may be that committee dynamics are so severe that even Jesus Christ Himself would be rejected as the person they need to walk on water for the company.

I witnessed dysfunctional committee dynamics first hand. Marshall had been working for Ralph since the company began. Ralph valued loyalty, and Marshall wanted to tout himself as the most loyal of them all. Some in the office joked that Marshall's loyalty was a bit creepy as Marshall would even visit Ralph's estate during the middle of the night just to bring him a report. Some joked that if it were possible, Marshall would have Ralph's baby.

Marshall's title is Chief of Staff, but what he does is keep a list of infractions that everyone commits against the company, such as leaving early or misusing company resources. I didn't want him on the committee, but I had to put him there because excluding him would certainly cause my hire to be placed on hold or sent out to another committee.

When Carol conducted a committee excluding Marshall, her hire met resistance from Human Resources who had Carol go back through the process. When the committee process failed the second time, she found out that Marshall had some concerns about the process. When Carol finally let Marshall become a part of the committee, the process went through and Carol was allowed to hire her person.

The more members on the committee, the greater the likelihood that dynamics prevail. So what do you do if you are in an interview where committee members don't like each other? And how do you spot those committees with dysfunctional dynamics in the first place?

Strategy #6: Appease the most toxic committee member

Your first job when you sit down for an interview is to see if there are any dynamics within the committee. You do this by paying attention to the body language between committee members. BusinessBalls.com lists a number of ways to identify dysfunctional dynamics as soon as you walk into the room. These include:

- Not all committee members are present because someone is late or had to step out of the room.

- One member is talking over another before the interview starts.

- Members look like they are reading your resume for the first time as you are sitting down because they did not discuss it ahead of time.

- One person is "giving the eye" to another.

- One or more members are fidgeting as if they can't wait until this is over.

- There is a sudden and eerie hush in the room as soon as you walk in.

If you notice any of these dynamics, then your next step is to identify the one person in the committee who is the most toxic. You usually can tell who this person is because they usually display one of these signs:

- They are sitting back in their chair with their arms folded.

- They spend time looking at their phone during the interview.

- They stare off into the distance.

- They ask a toxic question that they know has a 99% no-win answer for (i.e., *Tell me something about yourself that might make me not want to hire you.* Yes, I've used this question myself.)

- They sigh heavily at inappropriate times during the interview.

- They correct other members, and even you, about nonessential issues.

Now that you realize that you have a dysfunctional committee on your hands and you've identified the most toxic committee member in the room, what do you do?

Instead of blowing it off as something that is what it is, here's what you do: engage the most toxic committee member by asking them a series of questions that include:

- How long have you worked for this company?

- What is your role here?

- How does the role I am applying for interact with your department or job responsibilities?

- What are two of the biggest challenges that your department (or job) faces?

- If I was able to work with you to solve one of those two challenges, how would that help you?

What you are basically asking this person is if you can make their work-life easier. Would that be something that would interest them?

The obvious answer is yes. And if you do this, let me tell you what you've just done—you have just made yourself the #1 Candidate in the entire interviewing process.

Why?

Because your future boss (probably not the toxic one in the room) has just recognized you as someone who can not only work with himself, but who also can deal with their difficult co-workers. And everyone else on that committee will recognize this about you as well.

You don't have to wait until the end of the interview to begin asking the toxic person these questions. You can interject them during the interview. In fact, you should interject them as soon as you identify the toxic member.

Candidates who can appease the Marshalls of the world are valuable assets. You can make yourself valuable as well as long as you work committee member dynamics to your advantage.

The story continues...

So now Ralph's Hiring Committee was about to be in full swing. I figured that I had to do some politicking since I was officially the Chairman of the committee and also because I had to make sure that all my ducks were lined up in a row so that Jeff could be hired.

Before I made my rounds, I had to take a moment to consider the dynamics in the group—who liked who, who didn't like who, who respected who, who didn't respect who, and all that.

I had to admit that Marshall was the least favorite of everyone because he was seen as Ralph's pet. It would not be much of a problem if Marshall used his pet-ness to promote harmony in the office and advocate for the company as a whole instead of Ralph's ego.

I remember one incident when Ralph went on a tirade and set out to fire Stacy because Stacy's brother-in-law became one of our distributors. When Stacy drove up in a new car, Ralph thought that Stacy was getting a kickback and had Marshall find out.

Marshall did find out that Stacy's brother did buy her the new car, so Ralph fired Stacy for conflict of interest. Unfortunately, Stacy took $500,000 worth of business with him which Ralph never got back. I thought that I made a good case to Ralph and Marshall why we shouldn't let Stacy go, but Marshall was bent more on satisfying Ralph's ego than keeping the business in the company.

Since people didn't like Marshall, perhaps I should tell him that Paula knows Ralph's son. Then if Marshall sided with Paula, everyone else would be against her because of him.

But then Marshall would tell Ralph that Paula knows Eban and the whole process could blow up in my face. I need to let this one play out.

Marshall dislikes Becky the most. I'm not sure what happened between them, but some of his group email responses to her were a full-on misogynistic rage, in my opinion.

I couldn't have Becky fall in love with Jeff too quickly or Marshall might write Jeff off just to spike her. (No, I don't mean *spite* I meant *spike*, like impale her with a sharp point.) To be safe, I probably needed to play up Jamila to Becky in exchange for some future favor. But then I couldn't play up Jamila and not have Becky select Jeff. This was not going to be easy.

Gail was the friendliest of them all, but at one point in time she got upset and didn't speak to each one of us in the group, including me. Gail is the type of person who loves pointing out problems without offering solutions. I wondered if I could start poking holes in Paula and Jamila so that Gail would take it and run with it.

Mariano was the person that everyone could get along with because he focused on doing his job and making everyone else's life more productive. Whatever needed to get done, he was great at executing it. If it were just he and I on the committee, it would be a slam dunk (but then again, I probably wouldn't have written this book).

I could be the most transparent with Mariano because he was a company man, and whatever was good for the company as a whole, he was all for it. I felt that having him select Jeff would be no problem.

After going through my assessments, I decided to make my rounds to check in with everyone before the interviews.

Even though it was already posted online, I attached the job description to an email I sent to the committee so that they could prepare for the upcoming interviews. I was careful to point out that the job description had already been reviewed and approved by HR, had been posted to Indeed, and was on our site. I didn't want anyone to add their own two cents.

Turned out, I had no reason to worry. Not a single committee member replied to my email. In fact, they never confirmed they received it, even though I knew they had. Now I wanted to go around again to do one final check to make sure there weren't any questions before the interviews. Otherwise, I would run the risk of somebody, probably Marshall, saying that I never followed up on the job description and that I was making it difficult for the committee to function properly.

In making my rounds, my first stop was Mariano. The whole politicking thing for this process had me a tad annoyed, so I needed to start with someone who wouldn't pick up on my irritation and possibly use it against me. Mariano obviously didn't care about anything except getting the job done quickly. He probably wouldn't even look up from his computer.

I rapped lightly on his doorframe. He glanced up at me and, sure enough, his eyes went right back to his screen. "Mr. Ed," he murmured. "What can I do for you today?"

"I'm flying off to Tahiti," I said. "Cover for me? Should only be about six months."

His eyes flicked up once more before he realized I was joking and offered me a three-second-long smile. "'Fraid not, my friend," he said. "I'm thinking a more short-term favor."

"Okay," I said. "How about this instead: I sent over a job description for the Project Manager position. I just wanted to see if you had any questions before our interviews next Wednesday."

This time he didn't look up. "Ah, yes," he said. "I remember. I did get that email. Truth be told, whoever you need I like, so if you're fine with it, I'm fine with it."

"Works for me!" I said. "Thank you, sir." I knew he'd say essentially that. There was no way he even opened my email. But I wasn't looking for pushback. That was for sure. I wanted to make sure no one disturbed the process so I could hire Jeff right away.

I made my way to Becky's office. "Hi Becky! How's it going?"

"Good morning, Edwin!" she smiled, her eyes crinkling slightly.

I decided to get straight to it. "Listen," I said. "I'm just stopping by to make sure you got that job description? We're doing interviews next Wednesday."

"Job description?" Her expression was blank and briefly, I thought, *I did send it to her, didn't I?*

"Yes Becky, the job description for the Ecommerce Project Manager?" I prodded.

"Oh, right," she uttered a tinkly laugh. "Yes, I received it. I was only kidding."

"Cool. Any questions or concerns?"

"Oh. Uh…" She looked at me, probably wondering if there was a way she could ask a favor in exchange for reading the description. Instead, she just said, "No, no concerns," and gave me her smile again. She wanted something I know so I had to get out of there quickly.

"Okay," I said. "Thank you much. Have a good one!"

I kept my voice light and friendly, but I had to admit my hackles were a bit raised. Did any of them even glance at it? I mean, it would be nice not to get any pushback, but I had a feeling it would still come, just much later. And I wasn't interested in finding out right before the interview that they all thought we needed someone with more experience, or with less experience, or someone who was a Scrum Master or something. Oh well. I gotta shelve my annoyance and get ready to schmooze with Gail.

"Miss Gail!" I exclaimed as I walked to her doorway. "You're looking lovely this morning."

"Oh, you," She flapped a hand at me.

"How's the college-bound grandson?" I asked.

After five minutes of hearing about his first choices, safe schools, and various majors he would be perfect for, Gail took a breath and I plunged forward.

"Oh, I meant to ask you," I said, trying to make it appear I just came over for chit-chat and something popped into my mind. "I sent out the job description for the Project Manager interviews next Wednesday. I just wanted to follow up, make sure you saw it, and see if there are any questions I can answer?"

Her face went blank for exactly two seconds, then she began nodding. "Yes, I got it. It looks pretty good."

"Okay, great."

"And you ran it by HR?"

I was tempted to point out that I already answered that question profusely in my email, but I bit my tongue. It was best, I learned, to keep on Gail's good side. She wasn't one for sarcasm. "Absolutely." I flashed her a winning smile, hoping she would ignore the exasperation in my too-loud tone.

"Good." She beamed. "Then I've got no concerns."

I waved and stepped out. Great, I thought. Not only was I annoyed, but I was also feeling insulted by Gail's pedestrian question, and now I got to go see Marshall. I briefly considered leaving him till the end of the day, but I could just imagine his reaction if someone else on the committee mentioned that I had gone around and asked everyone's opinion but his. He would probably spend days tearing my job description apart and convincing Ralph to let him create a completely different one.

I sucked it up and went to flush out that little troll from under his bridge. (Can you tell that I'm not too fond of Marshall?) Barely managing to refrain from making a rude gesture directly into one of the cameras as I passed by his assistant's cubicle, I knocked on his open door. "Good morning," I said.

"Edwin," he replied, sitting back in his chair a bit. "What can I do for you?" Like Mariano, the man got right to it. I could appreciate that.

"I'm just checking in with everyone to see if there are any questions or concerns about the job description I sent out? I've already run it past HR but I'm just checking in before interviews next Wednesday."

"Hmmm." He brought his hands together under his chin. "Have there been any concerns from the others?"

"None at all," I lied smoothly just a tad. For some reason, I felt as if I shouldn't let on that I went to him last. He nodded, satisfied.

"It looks fine to me," he replied.

"Thank you." I turned and left before he could see my shocked expression. Not even Marshall read the damn job description! I could tell by the look on his face, that sort of "deer in headlights" look people sported when they were asked to remark on a subject they knew nothing about. I kind of expected that nobody else would read it, but I was certain Marshall would have a few thoughts. At the very least, he would object to my using an eleven-point font.

Honestly, I wasn't asking that much of any of them. I knew we were all busy, but I could find the time to read a job description that barely fit half a page. Why couldn't they? I could feel my irritation bubbling to the surface and I knew it was partly because I spent a lot of time carefully crafting the description so Jeff would look like the perfect candidate.

I told them that I was scheduling half-hour interviews because HR, Gail and I had already done a significant amount of background work so that they didn't have to utilize too much of their precious time. However, I really shortened the interviews as a shotgun approach to hiring Jeff. I thought that the less time they spent with each candidate, the better.

I was worried that any one of them would screw it up by deciding later to actually look at my email and provide comments. It wouldn't matter that the job had been posted for a month or even a few days. Someone on the committee could ask me to add to it or question why I wrote what I did. None of them would have any problem giving me flack for a job description I wrote for a candidate who I would be their direct report and who would likely not do anything but make their lives easier.

The whole situation seemed sort of unfair, and once again, I felt annoyed with Ralph for forcing this committee thing on me in the first place. But I needed to shake off this negativity. To keep Jeff from slipping through the cracks, I needed to refocus and work in order to hone my plan to get him in the door.

Secret #7: During the Interview

There are obviously some interview do's and don'ts, but I'd like to start out with some interview mishaps from the HR Daily Advisor (/HIRING23) that some people thought were all right, but in fact were all wrong and cost them the job:

- Candidate took a family photo off of interviewer's desk and put it into her purse.
- Candidate started screaming that the interview was taking too long.
- Candidate said her main job was being a psychic/medium and tried to read interviewer's palm, despite interviewer's attempts to decline the offer.
- When asked what her ideal job was, candidate said "painter of birdhouses." (Company was hiring for a data entry clerk.)
- Candidate sang her responses to questions.
- Candidate put lotion on her feet during the interview.
- When asked why he wanted the position, candidate replied, "My wife wants me to get a job."
- Candidate started feeling interviewer's chest to find a heartbeat so they could "connect heart to heart."
- Candidate had a pet bird in her shirt.

- Candidate took phone interview in the bathroom – and flushed.

We could all laugh at this and shake our heads, but the reality is that all of us have our own ideas of what we think we should do and say during the interview. We take into the interview what we think will work, but then we get rejected for the job and don't understand what went wrong.

The reason this happens more often than not is because Hiring Committees have a mindset about the interviews in the first place that they never share with candidates: interviews are a necessary evil.

They are necessary because human resources are needed for customer service and to increase the bottom line; they are evil because they take away from the company's most valuable resource: time.

Most Hiring Committee members would rather be doing their own work than be interviewing you. This is especially true if you committed one of those bullet point faux pas listed above—you were just a big waste of time.

But what can you do about it? Ergo, Strategy #7.

Strategy #7: Offer to give back the time

Wait a minute, what? What are you saying? Offer to give back the time?

Yes.

At some point, the interview will wind down and they will ask you if you have any questions. Go ahead and ask them your standard questions (/**HIRING21**) about the job and their company but then ask them a question like this:

I know that you all are busy professionals and would probably prefer spending this time working on your to-do list or another one of your projects. I am thinking that you have spent 2 – 4 hours of your time in preparation for and with this interview. I would like to ask if I can give you back the time you spent with me today. Would you allow me to do that?

At this point you will have their full attention. Since time is life's greatest commodity, an offer to get back some time is intriguing.

When they ask you what do you mean, let them know that you are offering to take on a task or an unfinished project that they have and that you are willing to give up to four hours of your time to help complete whatever project or task that they have. You want to offset the time they had to take with you so that they could be more productive with whatever else they have to do.

And let them know that you are doing this on a totally volunteer basis. Then pull out a standard volunteer agreement like the one below.

VOLUNTEER APPLICATION FORM

PLEASE COMPLETE THIS FORM IN BLOCK CAPITALS

Name:	Male / Female (delete as appropriate)

DOB:	Place of Birth (Town and Country)

Address: ....

....

.... Post Code ....

Email address:

Telephone	Mobile

Do you have your own transport:	Yes ☐ No ☐

Are you currently a student?	Yes ☐ (full or part time) No ☐

Are you currently employed?

If yes, where and in what capacity: ....

....

....

Please give your NI No:

Have you previously served with the armed forces?	Yes ☐ No ☐

Do you have a disability?	Yes ☐ No ☐

(if yes please give details): ....

....

Please give a summary of your past work experience: ....

....

....

Please give a summary of your previous voluntary work, if any: ....

....

....

....

Let them know it doesn't matter what task it is, you are willing to do it to offset the time they had to take to interview you. Also let them know that after the four hours are completed according to the agreement, you will have fulfilled your desire to give them back the time they used to interview you.

You will have several reactions in response to your offer. I have only heard this once in my committee life and it blew me away. I took the candidate up on their offer, had them work on a project to help me get organized, and after the four hours hired them for a different position than they applied for.

Ever since, I have been giving participants in our job information workshops this strategy and the response has been overwhelmingly positive. Some people kindly refuse, but they never forget the offer. I have had one participant, Eric, tell me that the interview didn't go well, so Eric acknowledged that at the end of the interview and admitted to the committee that he just wasted their time and feels obligated to pay the time back using the method I just stated.

Eric was so politely insistent on helping them recover their human resources that he suggested several areas where he would volunteer for an entire day based upon their duties on the job announcement. Although they kindly said no during the interview, after he followed up several times making the same offer, one of the committee members took him up on his offer and used him for a small project.

Eric did such a great job on the project that although he did not get the job, he did receive a recommendation letter from the committee member. Eric then told this story on another job interview and impressed them so much that they hired him.

Your goal in this strategy is to get your foot in the door however possible. Once you do that, you are more inclined to get the job. At least no one on the committee will ever forget about you. So practice and develop Strategy #7. You are sure to get positive results as well.

The story continues...

In the two weeks leading up to the interview day, I spent time with HR creating the list of interview questions. Some of the phone screen questions would be included in the in-person interview because the committee might like to hear their answers. For example, we would ask the candidates to describe their current jobs, to explain why they were leaving their employers, and to discuss a challenging obstacle in their jobs that they had to overcome. On top of those, we would add the following interview questions:

- What type of environment are you most comfortable with?

- Describe an interaction with a difficult co-worker and how you overcame your issues.

- What type of management style do you most prefer?

- Tell me about your greatest work achievement (so far).

- If you were chosen for this position, what three areas of our company do you think you could improve?

- Say a project you're leading has gone off course: communication has fallen off, colleagues aren't completing the tasks assigned, people are skipping meetings or failing to report their current status. What steps would you take to get everyone back on track?

- How do you think your current boss and colleagues would describe you?

- Tell us why you think you'd be the perfect fit for this position.

Obviously, the interviewee's answers could invite other questions, but the ones I listed were what we wanted to get answered by anyone we were seriously considering for the job.

I had asked the committee if they had time to get together for a quick prep session a day or two before the interviews. I wanted to use that time to see if there were any potholes against Jeff. Of course, my request was met with a chorus of negative responses, so I scheduled the prep session for a half hour before Jeff was set to come in.

Mariano walked in five minutes late, so already we were scrambling for time. I went over the job description, the notes from Gail's and my telephone interviews, and my list of interview questions. I had sent all this information to everyone at least three times by now, but I was willing to bet some of them were looking at it for the first time.

"Are there any questions you guys feel like you want to ask the candidates?" I said. My question was met with silence. Mariano's eyes were down. He was clearly looking at his phone in his lap. Marshall was not bothering to hide anything – he kept the phone right on the table while he scrolled through it.

"Alright people," I said, hoping my irritation wasn't too obvious. "I mean, I do love the sound of my own voice—usually when I'm singing in the shower, but I do need your input, too. I'm relying on this committee to help me make a decision." *No, I'm not*, I thought. *But Ralph thinks I am, and I don't need anyone to go crying to him and claiming that I'm not playing nice.*

Gail cleared her throat. "Well," she said, "I personally always like to ask the questions about overcoming obstacles or a particularly difficult co-worker."

"I think I should tackle the difficult employee question, as well as questions about the management preferences of the candidates," Marshall said. "I like to get an idea of how these candidates will interact with our staff."

Hopefully better than you do, I thought. Out loud, I said, "That okay with you, Gail?"

"Well…" Gail appeared to be thinking it over.

Marshall went on, "The Project Manager has to interact with a lot of people here, people at different pay grades, if you will. I want to make sure whoever we bring in can handle getting along with someone who isn't carrying out the tasks they have been assigned, whether it's a director or a junior employee."

Gail nodded. "I suppose that's okay," she said, but her face didn't agree.

"Excuse me," Becky piped up. "I was hoping I could ask the question about overcoming the difficult challenge."

"Why you?" Gail asked, a tad accusatory, in my opinion.

"Well, it gives good insight about how the candidate handles problems outside of just employee conflicts," Becky said.

"Exactly," said Gail. "And since I deal with client relations, I think it only makes sense that the question comes from me."

Neither one of them appeared to be backing down, so I consulted my list of questions. "Becky," I said, "How about you tackle the question about the work environment and maybe the one about how they think they can improve our company or policies? I think those answers could provide some insight about how the candidates deal with challenges at work. Especially if they have to report to me," I added, trying to keep the mood light.

Becky smiled slightly. "Okay, Edwin, sounds good," she agreed. I could tell she was not happy, but she would probably think of a way I could make it up to her later. Maybe I'm just overreacting about Becky always wanting a quid pro quo… and maybe not.

Marshall opened his mouth, no doubt to disagree with Becky, so I quickly added, "Marshall, I'm hoping you wouldn't mind also asking why the candidates think they'd be perfect for the position. I think that question deserves your shrewd attention." Of course, I was buttering him up, but it seemed to work because he shrugged and said, "Fine."

"Mariano?" I said. "Anything you want to take on?"

Mariano glanced up, obviously not listening. "No thanks, Edwin," he said. "I like to observe and listen. I think the rest of you got it under control."

"Edwin," Marshall said, "Why don't you ask some questions pertaining more to the project, like…" he paused as he glanced down at the questionnaire. "Like, this question about how they'd get a project that is running off the rails back on track. And maybe you could ask about their technology backgrounds, since they'll be training people on the systems."

"Absolutely," I replied. "That makes sense. I want someone who can get the job done without having to ask me for help every five minutes." I almost went on to say I picked Jeff for this reason, but that will only serve to make everyone suspicious. If Marshall thought

I was gunning for a particular candidate, he might get concerned that Jeff was a buddy and I was throwing him a bone, or that Jeff and I planned to join forces and overthrow Ralph.

Overall, it felt like my prep meeting wasn't going well. Everyone went from being totally silent to wanting to ask the same question, then got somewhat pouty when they weren't getting their way. The temperature of the room seemed to have dropped with all the cold looks being thrown around, and I couldn't have everyone feeling irritated and snappish when Jeff came in.

This was actually quite funny to me in a way. Here we were all pretending that we cared about a process that we really didn't care about that much. I didn't care to go through it and just wanted to hire Jeff outright, and everyone else didn't care because they all had something better to do. But here we were, acting like people who cared but really didn't. This was kind of funny to me—not funny ha-ha, but funny in an inconvenient way, like always having to laugh at your boss's boring jokes.

In an effort to thaw the freeze, I said, "I gotta say, being in this room always gives me PTID: Post-Traumatic Interview Disorder. It reminds me of some of the intensely awful interviews I have conducted over the years. There's this one in particular I did, I think it was a couple years ago now. The guy, well, he was practically a kid, really – he'd been out of college only a few years, but he had good experience. When he came in, he was dressed nicely, but he was so nervous he sweated through his shirt and suit jacket."

"Woah!" Gail said.

"Poor guy," Becky said.

"Yep. I could see big stains on his shirt because they'd spread almost to the front. But that's not why we passed. When I asked if he had questions, he asked how much we were paying. I was a little taken aback because, you know, it's sort of an unspoken rule that you don't touch salary until a position has been offered to you. That's my feelings on the subject, anyway. But I went with it, and I quoted a range and asked if he was comfortable with it. He replied, 'Hmmm. Not sure. I'll need to ask my dad.'"

"His *dad*?" Gail's mouth dropped open.

"Yes. I had to ask him to repeat himself because I thought I'd misheard him. Turns out, his dad negotiates salaries for him. He actually asked if I wouldn't mind calling his dad to talk it over."

Gail gasped, her hand theatrically over her mouth. Becky laughed her little tinkly laugh. Even Marshall looked amused.

"How does someone like that get hired *anywhere*?" Gail asked.

"No clue." I shrugged. "Needless to say, I declined, both to contact his father and to offer him the job. And his resume went right into the shredder."

Becky and Gail laughed, and Marshall's smile widened. Mariano looked up at the noise and smiled slightly, like people do when they missed the punchline but feel like they should react.

"How about the rest of you?" I asked. "Any, um, *interesting* interviewing experiences?"

My little trick was working. Everyone seemed to forget about how annoyed they were as they told stories about their interviews. A lot of the stories revolved around nervous candidates – Gail even told us about a friend of hers who interviewed someone who was so distraught she *threw up* on the table. I hoped these tales reminded this room of busy, important directors that we were all just humans, and at one point, we were all that sweaty, nervous kid who just wanted a job. But maybe we knew a bit better than to have our parents try to negotiate for us.

Just then, there was a knock at the door. Connie stuck her head in. "Jeff is here," she told us.

"Thanks, Connie. Send him in," I said.

Jeff entered, sharply dressed in a dark suit, all smiles and firm handshakes. The committee members, still riding the high from their interview stories, greeted him warmly and made small talk for a bit before jumping into the nitty-gritty.

It was glorious. Jeff was amazing – funny and witty, but sharp and intelligent. He gave serious thought to the questions and answered them thoroughly without uttering a single "um" or "I'm not really sure." He was gracious and humble and he never got flustered or tripped up, despite the fact his interview ran over the promised half-hour (which I told him would likely happen).

Since I told him that Marshall was the most toxic of the group, Jeff spent particular time asking Marshall some questions and addressing situations that would appeal to him. For instance, Jeff asked Marshall to name a task that he (Marshall) disliked, to which Marshall said he didn't like reconciling SKUs every year. Jeff then said as *his* (Marshall's) Project Manager, he would develop an automated process for reconciling SKUs because he had done something similar to that before. In fact, because the committee spent time out of our busy schedules to interview him, he would volunteer a full day just to work on Marshall's SKU project.

Marshall was pleasantly stunned. He would have jumped at the chance right then and there to get help on his SKU project, but I declined for the committee hoping that it would help make me look fair and impartial. Marshall seemed annoyed at me, which was a good thing in this instance, but as the Committee Chair, I had to move the process along.

Gail asked a few questions that weren't on the questionnaire, even though she never mentioned she wanted to add anything to the process. But I wasn't surprised or annoyed. Jeff answered them as easily as the ones I'd given him in advance. When asked if he had any more questions, he asked a few, all of which were the kind that make interviewers say, "Great question." I mean, even Marshall looked thoroughly impressed. Hell, even Mariano appeared to be paying attention! All in all, I'd say Jeff owned the interview. It almost seemed like we didn't even need to continue the interview process.

After he left, I exchanged knowing smiles with the other committee members.

"He seems pretty good; don't you think?" I asked.

"I think he would be an excellent addition to our team," Marshall agreed.

"He's pretty perfect!" Becky said.

"Yes," Gail said, shaking her head in disbelief. "He's almost *too* perfect."

"What do you mean?" Marshall asked before I could interject.

"He just was so... on top of things. It was like he'd been coached." I kept a poker face, but thankfully, she didn't look my way.

"Well, you all know I talked to him on the phone," I said. "And it's true, he had very good answers to my questions. But I just chalked it up to the fact that he knows our business, he knows ecommerce, and he's managed a number of projects in the past."

Marshall, Becky, and Mariano all nodded thoughtfully.

"Sure, there's no denying his experience," Gail said. "But I can't help but wonder: were we meeting with the real Jeff, or were we talking to someone who just knows how to answer the questions?"

Marshall looked puzzled. "What's wrong with knowing the answers to the questions?" he asked.

"That's not what I mean," Gail told him. "I mean, maybe he's just excellent at interviews. Maybe he knows he's talking to a committee of top-level people and he can schmooze well. But that skill does not necessarily translate into a good employee or leader."

Luckily, Connie entered the room with Paula in tow, so the conversation was put on hold. But I admit, I was taken aback. I didn't want Gail to repeat her suspicions that Jeff came across as coached. Otherwise, the others might start to see it her way and wonder why Jeff seemed so prepared.

Paula was very nice. She was a great conversationalist, which was a trait that I knew everyone on the committee appreciated. But professionally speaking, she was not the same caliber as Jeff. Her answers lacked the confidence Jeff displayed. The questions we asked about her project experience actually seemed to stump her a bit.

In fact, she had trouble recalling her own resume. When Becky asked her to expand on the projects she managed in Chicago, she hemmed and hawed a bit, as if she didn't understand the question. Truth be told, she sounded like someone who had never managed a project in her life.

Marshall was obviously not impressed because instead of asking his questions, he glanced rather pointedly at his watch and said, "Do you have any questions for us?"

Secretly, I was elated. I had been worrying about Paula for no reason. She clearly was not a threat. The committee wasn't even interested in asking her everything on the questionnaire.

"Actually, I do have one question," Paula said. "I'm wondering if this ecommerce project you are hiring for has anything to do with the Generational Equity partnership?"

I exchanged puzzled looks with the other committee members. "The partnership?" I repeated.

Paula didn't seem to pick up on my confusion. "I spoke to Eban the other day, and he said Ralph is planning to move in that direction. I'm asking because I've worked on GE projects in the past, so I'm pretty familiar with how they operate."

We fell silent as we tried to decide how to respond. It was obvious to me that the others didn't know any more about what Paula was talking about than I did. We all heard rumors that Ralph would possibly sell the company when he retired, since his sons didn't want it, but nothing concrete had ever came out of the talk. Now it sounded like it might actually happen. But why would Eban know about it when no one else in the room seemed to know? And why would he tell Paula?

Marshall seemed to have recovered. He leaned forward and said, "It's possible. Your mentioning GE reminds me: I wanted to ask if you would talk to us about their operational process a bit? Nothing confidential, of course," he added.

"Sure," Paula said. She didn't think it was odd to be in an interview for one company and get asked questions about a different business.

Paula's responses seemed to spark an interest in the other committee members. Becky asked her what it was like to work for GE, and Marshall even wondered if Paula could describe their buyout process. I couldn't believe he could be so bold, but again, Paula took the question in stride and had no problem answering.

This sudden interest in Paula was disconcerting, and I interrupted a couple of times to point out that we were practically holding Paula hostage, and to remind them that we had other appointments to keep. Finally, everyone finished their barrage of questions and we said our goodbyes.

"I liked her," Mariano said. My head snapped up in amazement. Of all the times he chose to pay attention!

"Me too," Becky said.

"I agree," Gail added. "I think she'd be a good fit here."

"I didn't like her as much as Jeff," Marshall said. I could've kissed him.

"Why do you say that?" Gail asked.

"She had a lot of good information, that's for sure," Marshall said. "But it mostly pertained to GE. She didn't seem to know much about project management, which is what we actually need her for."

"I'm with Marshall here," I said. Not too eagerly, I hoped. "I feel like she doesn't know much about these projects she claimed to have worked on. I think we need someone who can hit the ground running, so I'm not spending tons of time on the onboarding process."

"Why did you put it that way?" Gail asked me.

"What way?"

"Why say projects she 'claimed' to work on?" Gail frowned. "Do you think she's lying?"

"No, of course not," I replied, but that was exactly what I thought. "But did you notice how she didn't know how to answer questions about them? I mean, there were times when it seemed like she didn't understand what we were talking about."

"Oh, I don't know about that," Gail said. "It's true she's not a perfect interviewer like Jeff. Maybe she was a little nervous. Interviewing across the table from five directors can be intimidating."

Marshall shook his head. "Then she won't last here," he said. "She has to set up weekly meetings and speak to a group of more like fifteen people. She has to know what's going on, and she needs to clearly explain what is expected of everyone. If an interview with a five-person committee is too difficult, she's in the wrong career."

My eyes looked like I just arrived at Disneyland. Was Marshall just supporting my candidate? Was he really sounding like a Chief of Staff or what? I was almost shocked but had to come to myself and realize that it was still Marshall saying all that.

Gail pursed her lips a bit, but she did admit, "That's true. Maybe she just had an off day. On the phone she was more clear and had more confidence, I think."

Confidence like she had been coached? I wanted to ask. But I kept my mouth shut.

We heard a knock, and the door was pushed open. "Guys?" It was Connie. "I've got Jamila waiting out here. Are you ready for her? You're running a bit behind."

We'd spent forty minutes on Jeff, fifty-five minutes on Paula, and several minutes in between discussing both candidates. We barely had time for Jamila, but of course, that's what I'd been hoping for all along.

"Yes, Connie," I said. "Sorry about that."

When Jamila came in, we apologized for being behind schedule and got right to the questions. Almost immediately, I realized I might have been wrong in assuming Jamila wasn't a threat. She seemed like the opposite of Paula: on paper, she was mediocre, but in person, she was a whiz. When it was her turn to ask questions, she wanted to know about end users and stakeholders. It was stuff the others certainly hadn't thought of, stuff probably none of us but Ralph thought about on a daily basis. I could tell the committee was impressed with her. Hell, even I was impressed! I found myself thinking, "Jeff who?" for a minute.

After our standard questions had been answered, Gail asked Jamila her additional questions. To one she responded, "That's a good question, but I don't have an answer for that right now. And I can assure you, I am good at following up," she added, smiling confidently.

It's admirable when people can admit they don't know something, and I do like a person who will see a thing to the end and follow up with people waiting for answers. But Jeff's answer to that question was much more impressive, especially since he'd had an actual answer. Our project manager would need to think on their feet, and part of that would involve having all the answers (or at least appearing like you did).

When Jamila had left, the committee agreed to take a break and reconvene later to discuss our candidates at length.

SECRET #8: POST INTERVIEW

Most companies don't want to tell you that 84% of the time your fortune or fate has already been decided once you walk out the company door. In the yes-no-maybe world of post interviews, by the end of the day many committees decide who should be considered for the position and who should not.

Only a small fraction of committees operate in the *maybe* category. Why? Because having a bunch of maybe candidates means that the committee process must be extended, and most committee members don't want to take up more time reviewing more candidates or re-reviewing old ones.

So what should you do after the interview? That depends whether or not you think the interview went well. You can tell if an interview goes well if they start asking you questions about your availability and how soon you can start. And you can tell that an interview didn't go well if they stop asking you questions or cut the interview short.

If you think that the interview went well, you should follow up with every committee member by writing them a note or by following any instructions (/HIRING26) that they give you (such as waiting to hear from a particular person).

If you think that the interview didn't go well or you are not sure, but you really want the job, then you should employ Strategy #8 and get someone to pass along a message for you.

Strategy #8: Get someone to pass on your message

Let me begin by sharing my introduction to this strategy. Several days after participating in a Hiring Committee, my admin assistant comes to me and hands me a note from one of the applicants and says, "Here's a note from Jennifer who you interviewed on Tuesday. I kinda like her."

I said okay, took the note and read it. It was a standard thank you note, but the fact that my admin assistant handed it to me made the note's impact on me much greater.

Fast forward... Jennifer became the top candidate for the second round of interviews. She wasn't hired for the position, but because my admin assistant liked her, I recommended Jennifer to another co-worker who hired her. Jennifer worked out great for my co-worker, and when I ran into her months later, I asked how she knew my admin assistant. It turns out that she didn't know her, but sent her a note asking her advice about sending me a note. *Brilliant!* I thought.

Ever since then, I have recommended this post interview strategy to family, and friends, and workshop participants alike. Over the years I have refined this strategy from the feedback I received.

First. Understand that this strategy requires some detective work. Not too much, but just enough to get some readily available information.

Second. You need the email address, mailing address, or phone number of someone who knows the person on the Hiring Committee who would potentially be your direct report.

This could be the person's secretary, admin assistant, or co-worker. If you know who you would work for before the interview, let the person at the front desk know that you are there to interview with your potential future boss and wanted to follow up through his or her secretary, admin assistant, or co-worker.

If you don't know who your boss would be until after the interview, simply ask whoever is at the front desk for this information as you are leaving. Don't be afraid to ask because more often than not, you will get this information.

If you don't get it at the interview, you can always call back and request this information. Let the person who answers the phone know that you are trying to get a message to your potential boss's admin assistant. Be kindly persistent because this step could land you a job.

Third. Once you receive the contact information, here's what you say: *Hi Candice, this is Rob Ross and I just had an interview with your boss Stacy. I thought that the interview went well and I wanted to thank her for it. Can you do me a huge favor and take a quick look at my thank you note* *for her? If you think it's okay, then can you forward it to her (or give it to her if you send a hand-written note)? And, if you have any feedback for me that would make the note even better, I would greatly appreciate it. Thanks, Candice, for being my go-to person and I hope to be working with you soon. Have a fantastic day. Rob.*

You can make your own variation of the note. The main point is that if you enlist someone to pass along a note for you, that will help you stand out as desirable candidate.

Oh, and another piece of advice: only ask one person to send a note for you. If you ask more than one and you're found out, then you would be perceived as a manipulator, and that definitely won't get you the job.

The story continues...

After the break, we gathered together in the conference room again to hash things out.

"All right, everyone," I said, "We don't have a ton of time, so let's get right to it. Show of hands, who thought Jamila was the best candidate?"

Gail's hand shot up, and Mariano lifted his index finger.

"Okay. And Jeff?"

Marshall and I raised our hands. Good ol' Marshall. Over the course of a few hours, he'd become my best friend, but only until noon.

"Paula?"

Becky primly lifted a hand in the air.

"Well, it looks like we need to get aligned. Let's go around and make the case for why we chose our favorites. Becky, do you want to go first?"

"Sure," Becky nodded. "I thought Paula had a lot of valuable information. She seemed pretty sharp."

I suspected the "valuable information" Becky was referring to was the stuff she could use to her advantage.

"But like we said, her information was mainly about GE, not project management," Gail pointed out.

"I know," Becky conceded. "But I still think the projects she worked on in Chicago were impressive."

"I think Paula could be a liability," Marshall said.

"Why is that?" Becky asked.

"Frankly, she had no right to disclose that GE information to us. I mean, why would she think it was appropriate to discuss a possible partnership with another company when the CEO wasn't even present?"

"Well, you were the one who asked her about it, Marshall," Becky sounded a tad accusatory.

"So what?" Marshall asked. "I can ask all I want. Whether she chooses to answer or not is on her."

"I actually agree with Marshall," Gail said, which honestly surprised me a little.

"You do?" Becky was as shocked as me.

"She probably should've kept some of that GE stuff to herself," Gail said.

"She seems too… political," Marshall added. "And I'm still not convinced she knows as much about project management as her resume indicates."

Becky had been nodding the whole time Marshall was talking. "All right," she said. "I liked Paula, but if you all think she's not the right fit for this job, I will agree to drop her from the race."

"Well, I third the motion," I joked. "Mariano and Gail, what are your thoughts on Jamila?"

Mariano nodded at Gail, so she began. "I *loved* her," she said. Her eyes shone. "She knew her stuff, and she's worked on several very important projects."

She was interrupted as a series of buzzes and beeps from our laptops and phones filled the room. It seemed we all got an email at the same time. Mariano, whose eyes were never very far from his phone, checked his email.

"We got a mass email from Jamila," Mariano said. "A thank-you for the interview."

"Wow, that was fast," Becky said.

"Yes, it was," I said. "Especially since I didn't give out our email addresses."

"What a nice touch," Gail said. I felt like she was looking right through me. "Very thoughtful."

Briefly, I considered whether I should have Jeff send a thank-you email, too, then immediately rejected the idea as seeming too forced. I needed to nip this Jamila thing in the bud.

"Yes, it was nice," I agreed. "And I was also impressed by Jamila's interview. It was definitely better than her resume. But I still feel like she just can't compare to Jeff."

I took out their resumes and laid them on the table next to each other. "Why don't we look at their resumes and do a little side-by-side comparison. If you look at Jeff's projects, his are very involved, and his description of the work he did is thorough. In some instances, he completed projects ahead of the due date, and many of his implementations saved the companies a fair amount of money." I glanced up at everyone and was glad to see they were actually all looking at the resumes, instead of their phones, or computers, or staring dreamily out a window.

"When I read his resume," I continued, "I don't think there could be any confusion about what he did. But when I read Jamila's, her descriptions are just a little cloudier, a little off. I've been through her resume several times and I still find myself thinking, 'Okay, but what did *you* do? What was your role in all this? Was the project successful because of you or in spite of you?'"

"I concur," Marshall said. "I think she does a good job explaining what the projects were, but she doesn't relate what she actually accomplished."

Gail said, "Yes, her resume is admittedly weaker. It would've been nice to know some of that info. But some people just aren't comfortable tooting their own horns, even if they're supposed to be convincing someone else how great they are. And these projects are all team efforts."

"Yes, but she managed them," Marshall said. "So I don't want to hear, 'Rah-rah, we're a great team.' I want to hear, 'This is how *I* made our team great.'"

Gail didn't respond to Marshall. Instead, she looked at all of us and said, "We all saw her in person. She has great communication skills, which is imperative of any project manager. The fact that her resume just wasn't as well-written as another one shouldn't count against her."

Ugh. She had a point. "I agree, Gail," I said. "And I, too, thought she had a strong presence. But remember when you asked your follow-up questions to both of them?"

"Yes."

"Well, Jamila's answer was that she didn't have an answer."

"And that she'd follow up with me. Which is exactly what I'd want her to say."

"Really?" Marshall said. "That's not at all what I'd want to hear. When I ask a question, I want the answer."

Never have I felt such affection for that grumpy little man before. I could've kissed him right on his bald head and would dare somebody to call me gay.

"Jeff *did* have an answer," I added, hopefully more gently than Marshall. "Jeff came across as someone who wouldn't make you wait around for days or even weeks to get an answer."

"As long as I get the answer," Gail argued, "I am okay with waiting. Sometimes things just take time."

"My point is, Jeff can think on his feet," I said. "A project manager has to be able to do that. If they walk around saying 'I don't know' all the time, who is going to listen to them?"

"That's a good point," Mariano said. "And Jeff was a strong candidate. I could see us going with him just as easily as Jamila. Ed, since you like Jeff and he's going to work for you, then Jeff is my choice."

Gail was silent a beat longer, staring at Marshall and me. I worried that I was campaigning just a little too hard for my guy, and Gail would respond by campaigning even harder for Jamila. I looked around at everyone and sort of shrugged my shoulders.

"Well, we've got two strong possibilities for the job," I said. "And while we don't fully agree on them, we all at least agree the job is going to one of them, right?"

There were nods around the table.

"Then let's go with a majority rule. Show of hands: those in favor of Jeff?"

Marshall, Mariano, Becky, and I all raised our hands. YES!

Gail looked at us all, then shrugged and held up her hand. "He's not my first choice, but I don't think we'll be disappointed," she said.

Friends, if you've never tasted victory, I am here to tell you that I tasted it, right then and there, in that stuffy conference room. And, oh, is it ever sweet.

Secret #9: The Offer

When you become the successful candidate, the company will make you an offer. That's great for you and good for them. But, they don't tell you that they always make an offer that is negotiable. That's true, 100% of every company offer is negotiable. All of them.

Now, that doesn't necessarily mean to *always* ask for more money, because the answer might be no. It could mean, though, asking for a more flexible schedule or adding a particular training or working with a particular group of clients, and so forth.

It is rare to find a job that has every single thing that you want, so if you are offered a job that you like, help turn it into a job that you could love by countering the offer. And when you counter the offer, always counter up.

Strategy #9: Counter up the offer

What does it mean to counter up the offer? Countering up means asking for something more while offering something more.

Many candidates just ask for more money and that's it. Companies will sometimes give in and pay candidates more money, but then they will put the candidate under a microscope to see if the investment was worth it. And, candidates who only ask for more money and get it have their work load increased 56% more than those who do not just ask for more money. So, you can just ask for more money, but the tradeoff could be that you now work at a job you hate rather than one you like.

I always tell workshop participants to never just ask for more money and always counter up the ask with a give. And the give should always be something that will benefit the company *and* you.

Here is a real-life example: Amazon offered Ricky a job as Operations Manager for $60,000. Ricky countered up Amazon by asking for $62,500 and for them to send him through a Lean Six Sigma (/HIRING27) certification training which is a high-power training that teaches graduates how to increase company's efficiency thereby increasing the company's bottom line. Ricky told Amazon that the increase in salary request, along with the certification, will give him more tools to help implement efficient strategies in the job that he believes would more than pay for his salary, at least in the first year.

Amazon was so impressed with his counter up offer that they immediately gave him the increase, along with his certification request. Ricky knew that this certification was gold and would make him a more valuable employee at Amazon and in any future company.

In another example, Brittaney was offered a job as a Supportive Living Provider for $12 per hour. Before accepting the position, she signed up for a free Excel Spreadsheet course on Udemy.com. She then told the organization she would accept the position, with the stipulation that after she finished the course in 90 days, her salary would be increased to $14 per hour and she would be allowed to help with scheduling patients on their scheduling platform which is done in Excel. Brittaney told them that her added skills would allow her to take on the extra duties and train others on how to use the scheduler.

The organization was more than pleased with how Brittaney countered up the offer and accepted her counter right away. She also knew that by giving them that counter she would motivate herself to finish the Excel training knowing that it meant more money and a better opportunity to improve her skills and net worth for the company and for herself.

In yet another example, Andre was offered a job in construction for $15 per hour. His work day was from 7 a.m. to 3 p.m. He countered up by saying that he wanted to add an additional hour to his work schedule by coming in at 6am in order to work with the crew manager on setting up the site so the regular workers, including him, could get right to work and save the company time and money.

The construction company said that they would give Andre the schedule and evaluate it after 30 days. And after 30 days, Andre's counter up proposal worked so well that he got an immediate raise to $16 per hour.

Do you get the concept? To counter up, you need to offer the company something that they need which would also benefit you, in addition to money. Be sure to always counter up.

The story continues...

When I went to Connie's office afterwards, I was practically skipping. Everything went exactly as planned, and now I would get to reap the benefits of having the perfect person for my job. I almost felt as if I should write a book, so others going through the Hiring Committee process could benefit from my insights. Oh, wait! I just did that.

I rapped on Connie's doorway. "Ms. Connie," I said, "Thank you so much for your help. I think we found a winner!"

Connie sat back and grinned. "Well, congratulations, Edwin. I'm sure you're relieved to be moving forward."

"You're not kidding," I said, handing her Jeff's resume. "Honestly, we had some good people to choose from, but the committee decided on Jeff. It was actually a unanimous decision."

Her eyebrows shot up. "A unanimous decision in less than an hour? Edwin, maybe I ought to have you working for me!"

I laughed. "Ummm, no! Wait a minute… ummm, no! I think I'd rather go through hell with gasoline drawers on."

I waved goodbye, listening to Connie's laugh as I walked down the hall.

Back in my office, I fired off a quick email to Ralph, letting him know how everything went. The email was merely a formality. I was pretty sure Marshall or Gail had been checking in with Ralph at every single step in the hiring process. I still couldn't believe it was all over and that it had gone so perfectly. At times, I definitely had a fight on my hands and I was worried about everyone being swayed by Gail. But in the end, I had to admit that getting everyone on the same page – my page - was pretty easy.

By late afternoon, Connie had emailed Jeff his offer letter and background check authorization. His start date was three weeks from today. I was so psyched that I decided to get Jeff acclimated right away. I began setting up meetings for when he got here. I thought about shooting him an email but instead I picked up the phone. Now that he was in, I could actually call him at the office.

"Congratulations!" I told him.

"Thanks," he said. "And thanks again for all the help you gave me along the way. It made the process so much easier."

"Nonsense," I said. "I knew you were right for the job the moment the position became available. I may have coached you on the politics of the group and our company, but really, your overall skillset is what won them over."

We went over some company procedures and had an initial discussion about the project. I explained who he would be meeting with and talked a little bit about the process I liked to use when handling projects. Jeff sounded as happy as me and he was eager to dive right in as soon as possible.

He did mention that he wanted to honor his word to Marshall and said that he put a small counter into the offer that HR sent him expanding his role to include the SKU project for Marshall. I was quite impressed. Yes, it made perfect sense to do Marshall's project in order to get some possible kudos from him. At the very least, Jeff and I would be less of a target. I told him that was a great choice and would approve the counter when I received it from HR.

When we hung up, I realized I never actually sent any thank-you emails to the committee members. While I was tempted to say "Thanks for making my life harder by forcing me to do a lot of the work," I knew I had to mind the office politics and acted instead as if they had all done me a great favor. Oh, well – I got my way in the end, so I was good to go. I sent out a perfunctory email, then decided to pay them each a visit to thank them in person.

As usual, I started with Mariano. I thanked him for his help, and to my surprise, he actually looked at me, smiled, and said, "Sure thing, Edwin. I think you made a good choice with your new hire."

Becky acted kind of like she should take all the credit for selecting Jeff, even though she was all for Paula. As soon as I thanked her, she asked me for a favor. I chuckled to myself as I left her office. Typical Becky. Your hair would be on fire, and she would spend a minute thinking about what she could get out of the situation, if she helped you put it out.

Looking at it again, I have to say that I respect her for trying to gain leverage in any transaction. That's just business, and we all do it to some extent. Even me.

Gail seemed happy to see me, but she threw me off by launching into a series of questions.

"Congratulations, Edwin. I may have been outnumbered, but I think Jeff is absolutely perfect for the job," she said.

"Thanks." I beamed.

She shook her head. "Tell me, how did he hear about this job? Does he have an *in* here?"

I was perplexed by the question, but I just shrugged and said, "Gail, he went through HR like everyone else."

"But I thought you told me you had somebody in mind? Before we even started the hiring process?"

What the hell was she talking about? I feigned confusion, but alarm bells were going off. I had told Ralph I had someone in mind, back when he told me to get the committee together. But I made certain not to tell anyone else. Did Gail somehow overhear our conversation, or did Ralph tell her about it? "I think I told you that I had my grandmother in mind," I said purposely half-joking. "I told Ralph I needed someone and he told me to put it to a Hiring Committee. Have you and Ralph been having *Executive Meetings* without me again?" I asked trying to deflect her.

"Hmmm," Gail said, narrowing her eyes. "Maybe I'm misremembering it."

"Is there something wrong with Jeff?" I asked.

"No, not wrong. It's just that he seemed to know *so much* about this company. Did you talk a lot about us during the phone screen? Did he happen to ask how the rest of the process would go?"

"He sure did," I said, "only because I gave him and everyone else an overview of the company and the hiring process. I tried giving them anything they asked for to help them through this process." At this point the best defense, I figured, was a full offense. It would be better than trying to deny it.

"But what did *he* ask?"

"He wanted to know about the company, the project, and company politics, our resources, and any winning lottery numbers I could share with him," I said in a lighthearted tone keeping in mind that the process was already over and that it was best to have fun with it. Any over-explaining or over-analyzing would have been fatal.

But my mind was going wild, trying to search out exactly what Gail was getting at. "You are sure asking a ton of post-selection questions about him. Where are you going with this?"

"Hmmm." She continued to stare at me, so I figured she wasn't satisfied with the answer.

"Gail! Stop it! I like Jeff, we hired him, and that's it. I like that he was prepared for the interview. And him knowing things about us is more impressive to me than someone asking questions who didn't take the time to find out where they would be working, wouldn't you agree?" I asked trying to turn the tables.

"Yes, I suppose so," she said. But the look on her face seemed to say, *I think you're hiding something.*

I said goodbye and made my way to Marshall's office. If Gail suspected the whole Hiring Committee was a ruse to get the employee I wanted, so be it. She would be right, and it wouldn't matter, because I hired the best person for the job. *What's done is done*, I thought.

Marshall's reaction was a bit more dismissive, almost as if he had been studying Mariano's moves.

"Mm," he said when I thanked him. He looked up from his computer. "I just hope he works out." His tone was almost threatening, as if I spent all afternoon talking him into hiring Jeff when he was on board from the get-go.

I came back to an email from Connie letting me know Jeff had already sent back all the documents. We were moving at rapid speed, and I couldn't have been more pleased.

Secret #10: Screening and Background Checks

As of the writing of this book, Human Resource studies show that over 90% of companies conduct some sort of screening and background check, both credit and criminal. The reason given is primarily due to public safety.

These checks are usually not done until after the interview or when a job offer has been extended. These checks are usually done by national companies and companies with 50 employees or more.

Companies usually don't say that if you are a stellar interviewee and they need someone with your skills, quiet often the company will give you an opportunity to explain away your bad credit or criminal record, if it does not involve an area of fiduciary responsibility or public safety.

Allowing you to explain yourself occurs more often with companies that promote inclusion such as those in the San Francisco Bay area. One job posting for UC Berkeley, for example, states that they have a culture of inclusion of ideas, people, and points of view, and do hire people with criminal records.

Something else companies don't tell you is that many smaller companies (under 35 employees and mom-and-pop operations) just Google you and check social media in addition to standard reference checks as their entire screening and background check. They do that because extensive background checks are too costly and too time consuming.

Having said that, in this culture of fake news, more and more companies are not relying on social media as heavily as they once did. Still, social media is a tool that companies can use to conduct background checks.

Whichever company you apply to, you can definitely help your chances of getting the job by how you use social media after the interview. It goes without saying that you should check your own social media presence before an interview and remove anything that might cost you the job (**/HIRING28**),but after that you should definitely use social media to help your chances to get the job after the interview.

Strategy #10: Post your interview on social media

If employers are going to check up on you by social media, why not boost your chances of gaining favor with them by posting a positive review on one or more of your social media accounts?

For example, after Jacquelyn interviewed for a Health Educator position, she posted on her Facebook account how she loved the job and the people and appreciated the opportunity to interview with them. She asked her followers if anyone knew more about the organization, because she wanted to follow up with them and would appreciate any feedback.

When the organization saw Jacquelyn's post during their background check, they were impressed and gave her the job.

When you do this, you must be very careful to consider the following:

- If you get the job, people will now know where you work.
- Other people will know about the job opening and may try to apply there as well.
- Haters may contact the company and try to smear your reputation.
- The company may be concerned that if you post a good thing about them on social media, you may post negative things as well. (This concern would be lessened if you don't have any negative postings about anyone.)

If none of this concerns you, then by all means make sure that you post your interview on social media, saying something authentic about what you like about the job and why you want to work there. Doing so could definitely increase your chances of getting the job.

The story continues...

A week later, my good feelings got yanked away from me. I found myself standing inside Connie's office, beckoned there by a short, mysterious email she sent, and I wasn't loving the look on her face.

"Close the door, willya?" she said.

Oh, this is not good. Not good at all.

After I shut her door and sat down, she handed me a file.

"Your project manager hire? We've got to go with your alternate candidate."

"WHAT?!?!? Why?" I asked.

"He can't work here," she said simply. "Look at the file."

I opened it and began to read. My eyes widened and my stomach headed straight for my knees.

"Wow," was all I can say at first.

"Yep," Connie said grimly.

"I'm not sure what to do with this," I said. "Why are you sharing this with me?"

"So you can see why you cannot hire Jeff," Connie said.

You could've knocked me over with a feather at that point. Silence reigned for a few minutes as I racked my brain and searched my mind as to what in the hell went wrong. I felt like those YouTube videos entitled, "Never Celebrate Too Early," where players would make a last second basket or score a goal and start to celebrate, only to have the other team score with a fraction of a second left. I've seen it, and now I've done it. And it doesn't feel good at all.

"I see…" I mumbled, trying to think. Connie looked at me like she just informed me that my dog died. "I guess I'm just not sure what this has to do with Jeff.

Connie looked uneasy. "Come on, Edwin," she said. "You know why."

"So, is this what background checks are all about? I thought they were for finding people who sucked at their previous jobs, but this is what they're *really* all about? Weeding out the best candidate?" I ask. Irritation was slowly settling over me. I knew I was being kind of ridiculous, but I didn't want to lose my guy over someone else's dirty laundry.

Connie looked a little shocked. "Of course not," she said. "They are about weeding out the candidates who won't… mesh well here. Who might create toxicity here."

"I see," I repeated. "So how often does that work? I mean, how often do you complete a background check on someone and then clear them, only to find out later that they are toxic to the company? Would you say 1 out of 10 times, 1 out of 100, 1 out of 1,000?"

She started to answer, but I wasn't finished. "Because here's the thing," I barreled on. "In the last ten years, somebody's department, a certain somebody who shall remain nameless, had *eleven* candidates go through your background check and *six* of them are no longer here. And of the six, four were considered toxic to the organization." I shook my head. "And then *we all agree* on a candidate, but you say he doesn't pass your background check — "

"The company's background check — " Connie began.

"Oh, excuse me, the *company's* background check. So, when a candidate cannot pass the *company's* background check, we don't have any contingency to make an exception, or whatever, if everyone else has signed off on it?" I already knew the answer but since I had Connie's attention, I might as well try to make her feel my pain and acknowledge how stupid her little process was. It was not like he failed a drug test or turned out to be on the FBI's Most Wanted list. Yet, still, he was considered "toxic." So that meant my perfect candidate was out, just like that.

Connie's face was full of sorrow, but she was head of HR, so I wondered if she was just good at faking that look. Maybe I was the only one who was sorry about this news.

"I know you're disappointed," she said. "I know you wanted Jeff. But I felt I had to share this information with you, even though it is confidential, so you could understand what's at stake. I'm afraid that fighting for Jeff may mean you win the battle, but in the end you lose the war."

She was right. And she made me an accomplice now. I couldn't fight for Jeff, even if I wanted to. Ralph would find out about him right away – bad news travels at light speed around here – and he would promptly find out that I knew about it and still fought to hire him. Being on the president's bad side would not exactly bode well for me.

I nodded, standing up. "I'm going to go wallow in my misery," I said. "Thanks, Connie."

"I wish there were some other way," she said. But we both knew there wasn't.

I gave myself a day to lick my wounds before calling Jeff. I had no idea what I was going to say to him. Because Connie shared his background check in confidence, I couldn't disclose any of the information with him. Instead, I could only be vague, or try to get him to guess. But how could he ever guess what I knew?

Jeff sounded both disappointed and perplexed when I broke the bad news. "I don't get it," he said. "There was something wrong with my background check? I never had that problem with any of my projects."

"No, I know that," I assured him. "It's not anything like that. It's more of an…internal issue."

"Internal?"

"Yes. I'm sorry I'm being so vague. Unfortunately, the information was disclosed to HR outside of their regular background check, so it's being kept in confidence and I'm not allowed to discuss it with you. Which seems very unfair, I know, because it pertains to you. But it's company policy, and I could get in a lot of trouble."

"Of course. I understand. I definitely don't want you to get in trouble," Jeff said. "But I just… I keep wracking my brain trying to figure out why there's a problem."

"Sure, I get that," I said.

"All I can think is if someone had a problem with the way I did a job and decided not to talk to me about it. I'm not saying I'm perfect," he rushed on. "It's just that… all of my performance reviews have always been positive. I honestly can't think of anyone who has had issues with me or my work."

"I believe it," I said.

"And I don't know anyone at your company besides you, Edwin," he said. "So I don't know how anyone there would have anything negative to say about me. I did post on LinkedIn a number of glowing things about the interview I had, which I thought went great, and that would look good during the social media part of the background check, I thought. This is odd."

"I can assure you," I said, "I had only good things to say about you."

He laughed a little. "I sure hope so."

"Well, for what it's worth," I said, "I think you'd be a great fit, and the whole committee loved you. If it weren't for this little trip-up, we'd have no problem moving forward."

"Thanks," Jeff said.

"But unfortunately, because I need to fill the position right away, we have to withdraw our offer to you and go with our second choice."

"I understand," he said. He sounded like I felt.

We talked for a few more minutes, then I hung up. I sent out an email to the committee letting them know that we were not moving forward with Jeff and had decided instead to extend the offer to candidate #2: Jamila. I didn't expect anyone to respond, mostly because I figured they wouldn't even read the email, so I was a little taken aback when Gail replied.

Edwin,

I'm confused – why are you now choosing Jamila over Jeff? It seemed like you really liked Jeff.

Regards,

Gail

I decided to fudge my response a little bit. I was worried Gail would try to pry the confidential information Connie had shared out of me or use it as a jumping-off point to conduct her own little investigation. Sometimes, I think Gail should sniff out gossip for a living.

Gail,

You're right, I did really like Jeff, but he has decided to move in another direction. No hard feelings! Jamila is definitely a great candidate, too.

Thanks,

Edwin

My answer seemed to satisfy her because I didn't get a reply. I emailed Ralph to let him know we had changed candidates. I received an email from Connie, letting me know that she had sent an offer letter to Jamila and Jamila had already accepted.

As I had done with Jeff, I gave Jamila a call to go over the job details. She seemed to know quite a bit about the project, which both surprised and impressed me. Maybe she was so bothered by not being able to answer Gail's question that she decided to do a little homework on our company. The dread that had settled on my chest yesterday began to lift slightly. Perhaps Jamila would be a good choice for the job after all.

A week later I got an email from Connie saying that Jamila had passed the background check and was good to go. I breathed a sigh of relief and got to work preparing for her first day.

SECRET #11: THE ACTUAL JOB

Here's the biggest company secret of them all: the actual job that you'll be doing will not be exactly like the duties described in the announcement or in the interview.

Sorry, but that's the reality.

Why is that? Because company stuff happens and the only constant thing is change. You may start out doing what was in the job announcement, but know for sure that your job will morph into something else.

Companies never tell you everything that you will be doing because oftentimes they don't know themselves. They cannot predict what will happen in the future so they can't tell you what you will be doing six months from now. That's why you see things like, "Other duties as needed," in many job announcements.

But think about this: your job should change, because if it stays the same year after year, then it could be a sign that the company is stagnant and not growing. Others might say that being able to do the same thing for years is a sign of stability, but in this ever-changing technological age know that for most companies to be successful, they must embrace some form of change to remain competitive. This even applies to not-for-profit organizations and government agencies (there have been cities that have declared bankruptcy if you can believe that).

So what should you do if your job becomes something that you didn't sign up for? Well, you have two options; you can do the job or you can quit. I've seen people do both.

I've seen people who quit, and the funny thing about that, which is not so funny, is that those who have quit seem to have a harder time finding their next job.

I've also seen those (in the majority) who would still do the job. Even so, there are degrees at which you do the job. Some people do the job with an attitude of ingratitude (which eventually doesn't work out for them), while others change their attitude about change and go on to not only make the job work out for them successfully, but then excel in a related future job as well.

I therefore recommend that if the actual job isn't what you signed up for, change your attitude about change.

Strategy #11: Change your attitude about change

What does it mean to change your attitude about change, when it comes to accepting a job only to find out that it isn't what you signed up for? It means to prepare yourself ahead of time for the unexpected. It is to be purposeful by reminding yourself that all that glitters may not be gold.

Before you think that this is a defeatist perspective, you should know that job descriptions are not legally binding documents and employers can and do often add or take away responsibilities from any job description that they advertised and that you signed up for. So it's best to be prepared in advance if (or when) this happens to you. Here is the strategy that has helped others change their attitude about change:

- *Understand what the Job Description means to you and the employer.* Know that job descriptions are more like job duty suggestions and are not legally binding. Employers are allowed to advertise for one job and have you do another.

- *Lower your personal expectations.* If you get a job with a nice title that's great, but don't let that define you. Of course, give yourself a pat on the back, but if you go in thinking that the world must serve you, then you're setting yourself up for disappointment. You can lower your expectations by telling yourself before your first day at your new job to expect the unexpected; to not be shocked if things aren't what they seem; and, to roll with the punches. You will still be disappointed if the actual job is not the job you signed up for, but by preparing yourself in advance, your disappointment won't last as long (especially if you follow these other bullet points and Strategy #12).

- *Eat a slice of humble pie.* Even if you get a job as a manager, you still need to know how those you supervise do their jobs, and to be effective, the company may have you doing some of the grunt work so that you know how to manage. Be willing to do whatever job it is because that keeps you grounded and gives you legitimacy with those around you.

- *Don't pull the company on the carpet, at least not initially.* Don't tell the company, "Hey, you hired me as a bookkeeper, but you have me taking out the trash!" Companies don't like that at all, and if you do that, you might be replaced. And you never know that taking out the trash may be a part of your long-term training. Yes, it has happened, even at companies like Google.

- *Look for opportunities to do your job description.* If you are itching to do some of the duties on your job description, then evolve into them by offering to do certain duties. It is better to say, "Let me do that because it was something you hired me to do in the first place," rather than complain about being given duties not on the job description.

- *Be patient.* Wait to see if the job duties will come about. You don't know but your skewed duties could mean that you are being groomed for an even better position. You never know.

- *Tell yourself it is going to be okay.* The job and the job description don't define who you are. It's what you do. Tell yourself that everything is going to be okay and that it will all work out in the end. This realization comes from my personal experience with my own jobs and the conversations I had with my students, who went through job transitions of their own. When we've looked back at jobs that seemed horrible at the time, I and we now realize that the job was actually a stepping stone for something better. So yeah, tell yourself that it is going to be okay.

Your actual job may not match what you will do for the company. The bad part is your disappointment, but the good part is that you have a job that you can use to your benefit.

The story continues...

To help prepare Jamila for the project, I set up individual meetings with the directors as well as a group meeting. I noticed how all their schedules were suddenly more open, but they knew these meetings were for going over Jamila's responsibilities to them and discussing how to best integrate the ecommerce project into their departments. I guessed that the fact they would be benefitting from these meetings encouraged them to find some free time to meet.

Mariano told me, "Jamila needs to work on a logistics flow. Fulfillment needs to accommodate all the online orders we get."

"I'll need Jamila's help with the budget," Becky said. "She'll have to be ready to both create a projected budget and adjust monthly, if needed. She'll also be in charge of setting some predictions about annual production flow. If this ecommerce project takes off, it will have an impact on our logistics."

"Introducing ecommerce to the company means getting to know new technology," Marshall said. "We will introduce new systems to our teams, systems they never had to use before. Jamila should know these systems inside and out. It's imperative that we have a subject matter expert to lead training sessions and to provide guidance in case anyone has questions or issues. I hope Jamila is prepared to play that role."

"This project introduces the need for a new level of customer service," Gail explained. "We need to determine how we'll handle it. Will we hire new customer service reps? Should we outsource the jobs? The same goes for employees who handle issues with the website. I want Jamila to evaluate our needs and come up with the best solution. She's done this in the past, so I know she's more than capable."

I was busily scribbling notes but Gail's last comment made me pause and look up. "She has?" I asked. "I don't remember reading about that on her resume."

Gail looked stricken for about half a second before recovering. "She mentioned it in the interview," she replied.

"Huh," I said. "I guess I don't remember that." Which was strange because I have a good memory and I am excellent at taking notes while listening. It almost seemed as if Gail knew more about her than I did, which wouldn't make much sense.

"Maybe she said it during our telephone screen?" Gail added. "I can't remember."

I let it drop. Jamila would be here next week, and I had to worry about scheduling orientation, getting her a security badge for the front door, and gathering roughly ten pounds of new hire paperwork from HR.

I must say, Jamila's level of communication continued to impress me. She emailed regularly during the week, gathering information about the project. She never asked about her badge, or her orientation, or what she may need to bring to help fill out her paperwork. She stayed very focused on the job and her roles and responsibilities. In fact, she probably emailed me and the other directors over 75 times already, and she was yet to step foot through the door.

Her questions were so insightful that I felt confident she would not only hit the ground running, but she would also bring great success to this project.

Secret #12: The Job Transition

Congratulations! You got the job and now you've just started your first day at work. All of your hard work has paid off and now you get to enjoy the fruits of your labor by earning a paycheck.

Sit back, relax, right?

Well, not exactly. Although companies don't tell you that retaining good employees is a high priority because turnovers can cost them up to twice the employee's salary, they still fire people earlier in the probation period rather than later. They do this because the closer they are to the application process, the easier it is to find a replacement if you don't work out. Most employers hold their breaths hoping that you do work out, and actually expecting you to work out, but seasoned employers know that 12% of hires don't always pass the probation period.

There are a number of things you should do when starting a new job. *The Balance* lists 20 things that you should do in the article: *Top 20 Tips For Starting A New Job* (**/HIRING25**). Some of my favorite tips include:

- Endeavor to arrive early and/or stay late.
- Be mindful of how much time you take off your first year.
- Participate in office activities.

- Express gratitude.
- Take care of yourself.

Transitioning to another job does produce a certain level of anxiety, so having a transition strategy like the ones shared in this article will prove to be helpful.

What I often tell those who are transitioning to another job is to give yourself room to make mistakes. You are not expected to know everything, but you are expected to know much of something, and the best way to know more is to show up and ask questions.

One of the keys to a successful job transition is to keep reminding yourself that you are in job transition mode. This means that you approach every day like it's your first day — energetic, thankful, excited, inquisitive, anxious, curious, and full of hope. And although this is not a guarantee that you will not be one of the 12% who fail to pass probation, employers repeatedly give more opportunities for success to those employees who show up daily in this type of job transition mode.

But the job transition mode has two sides of the same coin. One side of the coin helps the employer know that they have a dedicated employee, but there is another side of the job transition mode that is designed to benefit you in the long run.

Strategy #12: Stay in job transition mode

In my book, *The Daily Job Transition* (**/HIRING24**), I discuss having a mindset where your current job is simply a transition for your next job. Having this perspective can actually bring greater job satisfaction and make you a more productive employee at work. In addition, it also helps prepare you, if for some reason things don't work out in your current job.

So here are some strategies that you should do to put your own daily job transition into practice:

1. Update your resume, LinkedIn profile, and every place you have your resume posted the day after you start your job. Then update it each and every month. Select a day like the first Friday of each month.
2. Have Monday morning meetings with yourself to set a goal that you will learn a new task or skill about your job.
3. If you've reached the skill capacity in your own position, look at other positions within your company where you can learn a new skill.
4. Every quarter search job listings like Indeed.com for similar jobs that you are doing.
5. Get trained and certified in a new skill that really interests you, even if it's online certificate training.
6. Start freelancing or open up a side business.
7. Leave work early one day a month to have a family day or volunteer at some organization.

I know that these six strategies may seem odd since you just started working at your dream job, but I can give you a written guarantee that if you implement these strategies, you will have a higher job satisfaction level, because you will know that your current job isn't the end-all-be-all, and you would reduce the anxiety level of future job transitions.

Here's one thing to note: the job transition rate for every person is 100%. Yes, it's 100%. Everyone in the history of the world has had to leave their job at one point or another. The transition rate is 100%.

What the strategies above do is help you with the job transition that is sure to come. I go into more details in my book, _The Daily Job Transition_, so please be sure to check it out.

The story continues...

Today was technically Jamila's first day in the office, but we had talked so much already that she seemed like a seasoned veteran at the job. I greeted her warmly and took her to Connie's office so she could fill out some paperwork for payroll. Afterwards, I started to lead her to her new office when Todd stopped me in the hallway.

Todd was a junior colleague working on the project as well, so I excused myself to briefly go look at his issue and answer some questions. Jamila said she would wait in the hallway for me, but when I walked out, she was nowhere to be seen. Puzzled, I started walking around, looking for her. I went back to Connie's office to see if she was there, but Connie told me she hadn't seen her.

Have I scared her off? I wondered, heading back down the hallway towards my office. I passed Jamila's office on the way and to my surprise, she was already in there, sitting at her desk, typing away on her computer. I checked the door again to confirm that her name plaque hasn't been hung. Nope, not there.

"Jamila?" I said.

She looked up and smiled. "There you are," she said.

"I was going to say the same thing." I shook my head in amazement. "How'd you know this was your office?"

She looked around and sort of shrugged. "I don't know," she said. "It just kind of felt like a Project Manager's office." She smiled again, and I returned the smile, mystified. It was not as if she helped herself to someone else's office, but still. What an odd thing to say!

"Anyway," she continued. "I thought it was best for me to get started right away. There's so much to do. I hope you don't mind," she added as an afterthought. She already seemed to think I wouldn't mind.

"No, it's fine," I said. Actually, I sort of did mind, but I wasn't sure why. "Anyway, I'm hoping you wouldn't mind taking a break to go around and say 'hi' to the other directors. They have also been eagerly awaiting your arrival."

Mariano, Becky, and Marshall all greeted Jamila and chatted with her a bit. But when we got to Gail's office, you would've thought I was reuniting best friends from high school or something. I knocked on Gail's door and she looked up, her face breaking into a big grin.

"There she is!" she shouted, getting up and coming over to us. She actually *hugged* Jamila, and to my even greater surprise, Jamila didn't act as if this was the strangest thing that ever happened to her at a new job.

"Hi Gail!" Jamila said.

"Welcome aboard!" Gail boomed. "Man, are we glad to see you!"

Jamila laughed. "Well, good. I'm happy to be here."

"So, have you been around to meet everyone yet?" Gail asked.

"We've been to see Mariano, Marshall, and Becky, so far," I said.

Gail looked at me as if she just noticed I was there. "Why don't I take it from here, Edwin?"

"Huh?" I said. I was just so surprised, I couldn't form a real sentence.

She linked arms with Jamila, and I fought to keep my eyebrows from raising off of my face. Gail's a very nice lady, but this was over the top. She was being extremely affectionate and chummy with this woman whom she had supposedly only met one time before. Was it possible they knew each other and Gail had kept it a secret? Gail had hinted that she thought I was in cahoots with Jeff. Was it actually Gail who was trying to sneak a buddy through the door?

"I'll take Jamila around to meet everyone else," Gail said. "I promise I'll have her back after lunch," she added, beaming at Jamila.

I glanced at Jamila, who seemed perfectly happy with the situation and not worried that she was being kidnapped or anything. "Okay, sounds good," I replied. I planned to take Jamila to lunch myself, as was my custom with new hires, but if Gail wanted to take her, who was I to stop her?

I went back to my office to get some work done. Around two o'clock, Gail emailed to let me know Jamila was still with her, and the two of them were going around to meet a few more people, then they planned to meet with Ralph and grab dinner with him after, if that was all right with me. Again, I couldn't help but be suspicious of this new-found friendship between Gail and Jamila. And what was this meeting with Ralph about? What could they possibly have to say that would necessitate a meeting and dinner? But again, all I could say was, "Sounds good!"

Over the next few weeks, it appeared my predictions had come true: Jamila was able to successfully immerse herself in the project from the beginning, leaving little for me to do in terms of onboarding. But I also noticed she was making changes to the ecommerce implementation plan I created. A *lot* of changes. Every week, we would have a one-on-one progress meeting, and I would point out something different, to which she would reply, "Oh, yeah, I noticed you had us doing it this way, but I just thought I'd tweak it a bit," or "I liked the way you had this set up, but I thought if we did this instead, we would see a huge benefit."

She was always talking about how her new ideas brought big "benefits" to the company, as if my work was throwing us into the crapper or something. I was glad she felt confident in her ideas, but I wondered why she wanted to change so much. And I had to admit, part of me felt affronted, because why did she think she knew what was better for our company? She was the new kid. I had been here for years.

During my progress meeting with Ralph, I tried to communicate my feelings in a roundabout way. Ralph was, of course, eager to hear about Jamila and how she was doing with the project. I told him she was doing great (because she really was), but that she made some changes to our tried-and-true policies and methods. I casually mentioned my reservations about Jamila's new implementations, but Ralph didn't seem to mind. He didn't appear to share my concerns and instead asked more about what Jamila said or thought.

"I have no problem with the way we've been doing things," he said. "But if someone wants to bring new thoughts to the table, who are we to criticize? Especially if they're successful ideas."

I smiled weakly. "You've got a point there, Ralph."

But the fact that the CEO wasn't bothered sent me on a bit of a tailspin. Did I need to be concerned, or was I making a big deal out of nothing?

One evening when I was leaving the office, I ran into Eban in the parking lot. I met Eban years ago at a work party. Ralph often threw parties at his house for the leadership team, and his sons would attend and chat with us. Well, they usually would come for an hour or so, then borrow some money for one of their own business ideas, and then take off.

Still, Eban and I had talked enough that we were on friendly terms. I suspected part of the reason was because he never asked me to invest in one of his businesses.

"What's new, Eban?" I shook his hand.

"Not much, Edwin," he replied. "Just trying to take over the world, one step at a time."

I laughed. He had many more steps to go, I suspected.

"Hey, I'm actually glad I ran into you," I said. "I wanted to say I'm sorry we weren't able to give the job to Paula," I said. "She was great, but Jamila really blew us away in her interview."

Eban looked puzzled. "Paula?" he said. "Who's Paula?"

I frown. "Paula, from your seminar work?"

"Seminar work?" Eban parroted.

"We interviewed her for a project manager position," I explained. "She said she knew you? That the two of you had done some small business seminars together? She actually said she talked to you, not too long ago."

Eban slowly shook his head. "Sorry, Edwin, she's just not ringing any bells for me."

I was baffled. "You've never heard of her?"

"Well..." he shrugged. "I don't want to say 'never,' because I've worked with lots of people. So if we did do a job together, it must've been a while back."

"Hmmm," I said. "Thank you, sir. I'll see you later perhaps?"

"Sure," he said. "See you."

I turned and headed back into the building. In my office, I pulled Paula's resume from my file. Nothing about it seemed out of the ordinary. Then I remembered she said she did some work for Generational Equity. On an impulse, I gave them a call pretending to look for someone with ecommerce experience who might have helped us with an initial valuation of our company, and the main desk connected me to their Project Director.

I spoke to a woman named Tammy, who said they didn't have any project managers named Paula, nor had they had anyone named Paula leave recently. She wanted to know if she could help and I said I wasn't sure. By this time, I had almost been expecting her to say that. I thanked her and hung up.

Did Paula fabricate her entire resume? I remembered her confusion during the interview and how I thought she sounded as if she didn't even know what was written on it. It was beginning to look like all our candidates had hidden information that I was slowly starting to uncover.

How could Paula say that she worked for GE knowing that she wouldn't pass the background check? This was getting beyond strange. I decided to call Tammy at GE back and probe her for more information.

"Tammy, this is Edwin again. My apologies, but I think that I am having a brain-fade on names. I just want to double-check and make sure that Paula isn't one of your project managers. I checked your website and didn't see her listed and just wanted to make sure."

"No problem Edwin. Yes, that is correct, we never had a Paula but we do have a number of other great project managers. Can I schedule one of them to sit down with you to continue the valuation?"

"No Tammy, I don't think so. My boss was sure that we had contact with someone at your company but the name escapes me, and nobody's name on your website rings a bell."

"We did have one of our project managers recently transition to a former client," Tammy said. "But we replaced her with this guy who knows computer programming, online banking websites, and ecommerce systems for banks and other companies. He most recently worked with a company that created online payment systems based upon PayPal. He has a B.S. in computer science and an MBA…"

"Thanks Tammy," I said trying to slow down her sales pitch. "Sounds impressive, and if we need a valuation I'll give you a call. Sorry for wasting your time."

"No Problem. Call anytime," Tammy said.

I was about to hang up and a question popped in my mind. "Just curious Tammy, what was the name of your project manager who transitioned to one of your former clients?"

"Her name was Jamila."

I almost fell out of my chair. Quickly, I thanked Tammy and hung up. I grabbed Jamila's resume and carefully reviewed it, line by line. She did many projects, but there was nothing on her resume that indicated she worked for GE. I nearly picked up the phone right then to call Jamila and ask her why she lied, but at the last minute, I decided not to.

I needed to think this through. I couldn't understand what Jamila's end game was supposed to be. Tammy said Jamila transitioned to a former client, so it wasn't as if she infiltrated us to steal company secrets or anything. In fact, she made a lot of great changes to the way we did things.

But she did lie, and there has to be a reason she did. I decided I needed to talk it over with Ralph, because I imagined Ralph wouldn't be too pleased about this information. But Ralph was already gone for the rest of the week, and this felt like a conversation we should have in person first thing Monday.

On the way back to my office, I swung past Connie's office and I saw that she was still in. I walked in and closed the door before she could say anything. I passed over any formalities and got straight to the point.

"Connie," I said. "Why did Jamila lie about working for GE?"

I had to hand it to Connie: she didn't look even a bit surprised by my abrupt question. Instead, she absorbed what I asked and merely raised an eyebrow. "Who did she lie to?" she asked.

"Everyone," I said. "She lied by conveniently leaving it off her resume. Which is odd, because anyone doing a background check would have access to her job history. And since you were the one who told me she passed, I assumed you did the background check and discovered her little secret. So what I want to know is: why was it a secret in the first place?"

Connie stared at me for several seconds, and I could see she was trying to figure out how to answer. "Well,

Edwin," she finally replied, "All I can say is, her background check did not reveal any concerns for the company. But the information contained in it is confidential. And I have no idea why her resume does or does not exactly line up with her job history. I'm not sure it matters."

"But it does matter," I insisted. "Because why didn't she just say it? I know she was there recently. Did she screw something up? Was she fired? Did she bribe someone here for a job? Connie, you gotta give me *something*!"

"Sorry, Edwin," she said. "But you know I can't do that."

"But you told me about Jeff," I said. "In fact, you told me some pretty sensitive stuff about Jeff. And you didn't seem too concerned that I would tell him what I knew."

She didn't reply.

"But now you know something you deem too confidential to tell me. I'm wondering how you decide what is and what is not okay to disclose."

Connie sat back in her chair abruptly and sighed. She seemed to be turning something over in her mind.

"What is it?" I asked.

"Okay, I'll just tell you." She leaned forward again. "Edwin," she said. "What I told you about Jeff? It did not come from some sort of informal HR background check. It came from Marshall."

"What?"

"It's true," she said. "Marshall's the one who told me and provided the proof. That's not the sort of stuff we look for when we're vetting a candidate. And whatever we learned about Jamila is confidential. *I* cannot disclose anything," she added pointedly. "But Marshall seems to know a whole lot about people, so maybe you ought to ask him."

I was speechless for a moment. Aside from me, Marshall had been Jeff's biggest cheerleader on the committee. Had he gone out of his way to dig up dirt on Jeff, just so I couldn't get my way? Or did he simply discover this information, thought it could put Jeff in a bad place with Ralph, and then saved him from the potential misery? Either way, I had to know, which meant I had to confront Marshall.

*****

First thing in the morning, I headed to Marshall's office. I talked a bit about the ecommerce project at first to throw him off a bit. Then I went in for the kill.

"I think Jamila's working out well," I said, "Which is great, since we couldn't hire Jeff. Oh, and speaking of Jeff, I wanted to thank you for saving his life."

"Pardon me?" Marshall raised his eyebrows slightly.

"I think we all know that if Ralph had found out that Jeff's stepdad had an affair with Ralph's ex-wife, things might have turned ugly in a hurry. Especially with Ralph's temper. I know if my wife left me and took my only daughter for some guy who ruined her and then dumped her, I would rather kill him as payback than give a paycheck to a guy who would be walking around my company as a reminder of the personal hell that I went through. Oh hell no! So thanks for saving Jeff's life."

Marshall looked at me passively.

I leaned forward. "Marshall," I said, "How did you find out that information, anyway?"

I could tell he was trying to decide if he should come clean with me, so I decided to stroke his ego a bit. Marshall had a classic Napoleon complex.

"It was really brilliant of you," I continued. "You saved Jeff, but you probably also saved my hide, too. For that, I am eternally grateful. And dying of curiosity!"

Finally, he said, "All I can tell you is I have my sources. But they are kept in the strictest confidence."

"Do you get intelligence on all the employees?" I asked. I wouldn't be surprised. Do I need to mention the nine cameras again?

"I think it's important to do my own vetting, when it comes to potential employees," Marshall replied. "It's just to ensure they will fit in here and not cause any problems. I've found that HR often needs help in that area." He smiled slightly. "I keep what I call 'conflict files' on potential new hires."

"Conflict files?"

"Right."

"Does Jamila have a 'conflict file' with you?"

"No," Marshall said. "I didn't feel I needed to. Jamila is not my concern; she's Gail's concern."

"Gail? Why would she have any reason to be concerned about Jamila?"

"I couldn't really say." He shrugged. "That's a different department."

"Marshall, do they know each other? Did Gail secretly campaign to get her best friend the job?"

Again, he said, "I don't have an answer for you, Edwin. I will suggest once more that you bring these questions to Gail." I knew he wanted to be rid of me, and I was happy to oblige.

"Good idea," I said. "I think I will."

But Gail wasn't in her office, and when I tried her cell, it went to voicemail. I waited another half hour and tried once more, but it went to her voicemail again. This was unusual for Gail. She was generally easy to reach. Even though it was Friday afternoon, Gail would still be answering her calls or at least calling people back.

In a fit of frustration, I thought, *screw it*, and I called Jamila.

"Do you have time to meet today, as soon as possible?" I asked her.

"I can't," she said. "I'm in Las Vegas through the weekend for work stuff. I'll be in next week, if it can wait."

What work stuff? I thought but didn't ask. Sitting around stewing for the next three days didn't sound like an attractive option.

"It can't," I said flatly. "But don't worry, I'll call you when I get to Vegas."

*****

When I told my wife, Denise, that I was flying to Vegas that night, she said, "Not without me, you're not."

Despite my preoccupation with the mystery at work, I laughed. "I suppose you want to come along, too?"

"It'll be like a mini getaway," she said. "I'll book the time share for the weekend. We can go to New York, New York, and have some of that Sicilian pizza you love."

"That pizza is reason enough to go to Las Vegas," I said. "Okay, let's do it. It'll surely make this work trip more fun."

After I hung up, I spent some time going over what I knew, trying to fit the pieces of the puzzle together. It was obvious from what Marshall said that Gail and Jamila were in cahoots somehow, but I just didn't have enough information to explain why they were or what they were planning to do.

I made dinner arrangements for Saturday with Jamila, so I figured I would confront her, then I would talk to Gail, and finally, I could meet with Ralph. Ralph needed to know what was going on with Gail and Jamila. I wondered if I should tell him that Marshall sabotaged Jeff. Well, maybe he didn't need to know about Jeff. He would most certainly want to know why Marshall would want to sabotage him. I didn't want to be the bearer of *that* news.

*****

Denise and I landed in Las Vegas around 10:00 p.m. As we were walking through the airport, Denise tilted her head slightly. "Look," she said. "Is that Ralph?"

I looked in the direction she nodded and indeed, there was a man with his back to us who looked like Ralph. "It sure looks like him," I said. "But I doubt it's him. Why would he be here?"

Denise shrugged. "For the pizza?" She grinned.

We got the bag Denise checked and made our way towards the exit. We passed an airport restaurant and I noticed the Ralph lookalike was inside, sitting at one of the tables. Only now I was close enough to verify it actually *was* Ralph. And he was having dinner with Paula!

I froze, unsure what to do. Ralph was a married man. Was he having an affair with Paula? Did he convince her to interview at our company? Wild thoughts were coursing through my mind, as I tried to comprehend why Ralph was in Las Vegas with another woman. And not just any woman – Paula, the one who never met Eban, who never worked at GE, and who might never have done any of the projects she put on her resume.

Before I could pull Denise in another direction and disappear in the crowd, she was walking towards Ralph. Panicked, I hung back within earshot and watched.

"Ralph?" Denise said.

Ralph's head snapped up. He appeared surprised to see my wife, but he wasn't particularly embarrassed or nervous. "Denise, hello!" he said warmly. "Fancy running into you here!"

"I know, right?" Denise said. "Edwin had some business to attend to, so I just invited myself along and we decided we should make a mini vacation out of it."

At the mention of my name, I knew I had to go over and say hello. I picked up our bags and trudged into the restaurant. "Ralph, Paula," I said, nodding at them. "How are you both?"

"Hi Edwin," Paula said. She, too, seemed perfectly fine being caught on an out-of-state date with Ralph.

"Hello, Edwin," Ralph smiled and gestured to the two empty chairs at the table. "Please, join us, won't you?"

Before I could protest, Denise said, "We'd love to, thank you." She sat and held her hand out to Paula. "I'm Denise, Edwin's wife."

"And his better half, by a long shot," Ralph chortled, causing the two women to burst into laughter. I smiled weakly.

"And this is Paula," Ralph said. "She's the new owner of R&G Enterprises."

Paula beamed.

Now Denise and I were both shocked. "You sold the company?" I said, incredulously.

Ralph nodded. "I did," he said. "It's time for me to pack up my ties and break out my golf clubs, like a proper retiree."

"But... when?" Just when I thought I had enough surprises for the day, I get hit with the biggest one. On my weekend getaway, no less.

"We just finalized it this week," Paula said.

Ralph smiled at me. "Edwin," he said, "I bet you have a lot of questions right now."

"Ralph," I replied, "That is the understatement of the year."

Everyone laughed. I was not quite ready to join them, so I just gritted my teeth and waited.

"Denise," Ralph said, "You may or may not know that Edwin recently interviewed Paula for an open project management position at the company. So it's understandable that he's shocked to hear she's now the new president."

Denise looked at us with big eyes. "That's quite a career jump, Paula," she said.

"No kidding," I mumbled.

"I'm sure it comes as no surprise that my interview was sort of staged, if you will," Paula began, taking a sip of her wine. I motioned the waiter over to get Denise a glass of merlot and a neat whiskey for me. I had a feeling I'd need a few more before the night was through.

"For the past few years, I've been scouting businesses to see if there is anything I'd be interested in aligning myself with," Paula explained. "I've been looking into R&G for a while and I heard from a colleague that Ralph might be interested in selling. Of course, I contacted him right away, and we began meeting, so I could get to know the business and decide if I was really serious about it." Paula's smile widened. "This restaurant has sort of become 'our spot,'" she said. "We often met here in Las Vegas because I'm here a lot already and Ralph won't run into anyone who might be interested in what we were talking about."

"Until tonight, of course," Ralph winked at us, and Paula and Denise laughed.

"While we were in the process of finalizing the deal, you came to Ralph, Edwin, and let him know you wanted to hire a project manager for the ecommerce project," Paula continued. "And I recently read an article in the Harvard Business Review about would-be CEOs secretly interviewing for jobs at companies they were thinking of buying. It's a way to learn more about the dynamics of the leadership teams and how they interact with each other and the employees. So I asked Ralph if he would let me go incognito and interview for the position, before everyone found out I was buying the company."

Her interview, for which we had spent time preparing, turned out to be fake? I didn't like that she used that time to spy on us. It felt almost intrusive. But I couldn't exactly tell my new boss that.

"So would you say you learned anything about us?" I asked.

Paula's face was inscrutable. "It was definitely an eye-opening experience," she replied. I had no idea how to take that comment.

"But why did Jamila get the job? I mean, she worked for GE but she never put it on her resume. Does she have anything to do with this whole" - I waved my hand – "thing you guys are doing?"

Ralph's eyebrows raised. "Impressive," he told me. HE then turned to Paula, "He found out about Jamila," he said leaning a bit over to Paula.

"I met Jamila a few years ago," Ralph said. "GE assigned her to a project of mine, one I was working on when I first started thinking about retiring. Before Paula and I met. I liked Jamila. She was sharp as a tack. I wanted her to come work for me. So I put Gail in charge of making sure Jamila got the job."

So that was why Gail acted like Jamila was her long-lost sorority sister. They had gotten to know each other secretly while putting Ralph's plans in motion.

"Well, why did you bother with hiring her when you were leaving?" I asked.

"I talked it over with Paula," Ralph said.

"I asked Jamila to come on as a change-agent," Paula said. "I hired her to start making the changes I wanted to facilitate in the regime, so to speak. When Ralph told us about the ecommerce project, I thought it was the perfect jumping-off point to implement our new ideas within the company. She's absolutely fantastic at her job. She's been a lifesaver through this whole process."

It seemed to me that Jamila's interview was another waste of our time. And Jeff's, for that matter. Which reminded me…

"What about Jeff?" I asked. "Was he in on this, too?"

"'In on this?" Ralph asked. He looked at Paula with mock amazement. "He makes us sound so… *diabolical*."

Paula shook her head at him. "He does, but we kind of are," she told him. She turned to me. "No, Edwin, Jeff was not a part of this. Actually, he came out of nowhere, and he was such a great candidate that…" she didn't seem to know how to finish her sentence.

Ralph looked at me, and his expression was somewhat sheepish. "Gail told us about how you really wanted Jeff, and she showed us his resume and experience. But she couldn't let it happen. *We* couldn't let it happen. So she made up some cockamamie story about Jeff's stepfather having an affair with my ex-wife and leaked it to Marshall, knowing he'd go straight to Connie and put Jeff out of the game."

I glanced at Denise. Her eyes were as big as our dinner plates. My job probably sounded more dramatic than any soap opera she had ever watched.

"So… that affair story. That was a fake?" My mind immediately went back to the difficult phone call I made and how disappointed Jeff was. And how I made him feel like he did something wrong so we couldn't hire him. I sighed deeply and took another swallow of my drink. Then I flagged a waiter down and asked for another one.

Ralph wisely kept his mouth shut.

"Edwin," Paula said. "I'm sorry about that one. We weren't prepared for a candidate of Jeff's capacity to show up. And I want you to know that I will personally make things right with Jeff.

What about me? I thought.

"So this little experiment was the whole reason for the Hiring Committee? You didn't actually want all the directors to help choose the new hire?" I asked Ralph. He nodded.

I turned to Paula. "Just out of curiosity," I said, "What did you learn from the whole hiring process experiment?"

She smiled at me. "Well, I learned who I want to keep on board and who I can definitely live without." She raised an eyebrow at me, but her expression was bemused so I felt I might be lumped in the former category.

"Are Jamila and Gail here with you two?" I asked.

"Yes," Paula said. "I have a branch office here in Vegas, and since I was here doing work, I had Jamila and Gail fly in to go over some business."

"And I tagged along to do some gambling," Ralph added, and the ladies erupted in laughter again.

"When is all this going to be made public?" I asked.

"It wasn't going to be for another two weeks," Ralph said. "But I'd hate to ask you to hold onto such information for that long, Edwin, so I think we can make it official on Monday." He looked at Paula. "Sounds good?"

"Sure," she said.

I looked at Ralph. He looked really content. He also looked 100% not sorry for the Hiring Committee and all the other anguish he put me through, the bastard. So I did the only thing I could do in this completely insane situation. I laughed and raised my glass.

"To Ralph and Paula," I said. "May they both get what they wish for, and not what they truly deserve." I grinned wickedly.

Everyone laughed and we clinked glasses.

After dinner, I called Jamila and left a voicemail canceling our meeting. Instead, I spent the weekend enjoying my time with my lovely wife and trying to put the madness of Friday night out of my thoughts. Occasionally, my mind would go back to the outlandish stunts Ralph and Paula had pulled, and I would get a little irritated. But what could you do? I chose to have a little more whiskey and laughed it off.

*****

True to his word, Ralph sent a memo on Monday informing everyone that he had sold the company and was retiring. His last day was Friday. The office's party planning committee managed to put together a little retirement party in the lunchroom on Friday. They served pizza and pasta from a great little Italian restaurant and got him his favorite cake: chocolate cherry cheesecake from the bakery he loves.

He made a lovely speech, thanking us for our hard work and dedication and telling us about Paula. "It's been my pleasure spending all this time with you," he said. "And now, I can walk out the door confident that I'm leaving you in capable hands." Then he said goodbye, and he was gone.

Just like that.

WHERE ARE THEY NOW?

It can't just end there, can it? I bet you're dying to know what Paula meant by her cryptic remarks regarding who will stay and who will go. Did she come in the door, guns blazing, firing everyone in sight? Or did she keep everyone, no matter if they were good employees or awful? Well, I'd hate to leave you hanging, so here's the update as of the date this book was initially published.

Paula and Jamila

Paula and Jamila, otherwise known as The Dynamic Duo, are building a thriving business. Their months of research and fake interviews gave them a lot of insight, so they were able to move in and immediately implement new processes. Paula has since changed the company's name to The HONI Group. That may be a fake company name I just gave to match the fake interviews they gave me.

Although the employees weren't happy about the transition, they grew into them as the company itself grew. Paula has proven to be a driven business owner, and her vision for the ecommerce division allowed the company to grow steadily, adding some serious cash to the company and making the stakeholders quite happy. As a director, I don't mind disclosing that our holiday bonuses almost made the crazy lying, and sneaking around, and nonsense worth it. Almost.

Jeff

My perfect candidate may have gotten a raw deal from R&G, but he definitely bounced back. Unbeknown to me at the time, the candidate that replaced Jamila at GE was Jeff. I should have known when Tammy talked about this great new Project Manager with PayPal experience and an MBA. It all makes sense now.

I learned that Paula had Jamila recommend Jeff to Tammy and Jeff was hired almost sight unseen. It must be nice to be in the IN crowd.

Oh, and I later found out that Jeff was offered a salary higher than what we were going to pay him. I'd say he landed well.

Mariano

Mariano is still the Director of Fulfillment for the company. He's happy being a company man. It's his bread and butter, so to speak. He thrives in his routine. If Paula ever closed up shop, she would have to use a crowbar to pry him from his desk chair.

Becky

Becky also made the cut, but she only stayed on for a few months after the transition. She decided to move on and started her own company. It's called MAI, and I can't tell you what that stands for either, if anything. But I can say she had made great progress, successfully negotiating several large contracts and growing her little startup into an impressive multi-million-dollar enterprise. It's obvious she has great business sense, but I'm guessing she also cashed in more than a few favors.

Gail

Not long after Ralph left, Gail also decided to retire from R&G. She had been traveling to Las Vegas on business and she fell in love with the city. I guess she has a thing for deserts and casinos. Anyway, she and her husband moved there and bought a huge house. Being an excellent cook, she renovated the kitchen and made it a state-of-the-art haven any chef would love to work in.

Gail was not one to sit around and feed quarters into a slot machine, so she decided to start a catering business and run it out of her home. She mostly makes gourmet food for networking lunch events. She loves what she does – she says she's "in her element" – but I'm sure she misses all the company gossip, which I suspect was an additional perk of the job.

Marshall

Alas, Paula decided Marshall was someone she could live without. He was let go from the company soon after she took over. He spent months trying to find another job as Chief of Staff, but he was unsuccessful. Because he was unwilling to look for anything else, he decided to return to Burma and go back to his career as a dentist. I'm not too familiar with the laws there, but I'm fairly certain he is not allowed to install any cameras in his office.

Ralph

Ralph has been enjoying the retired life, but like Paula, he can't seem to sit still for a moment. He has become a mentor to Eban, helping him with a new business idea. Instead of just being the wallet behind another failed enterprise, he's stepping in and showing Eban what it takes to run a successful company. Eban offered him a position in the company, but he declined and said he'd rather be a silent partner. Also, he wasn't kidding when he said he would be picking up his golf clubs – he is on the green nearly every day.

Edwin

And me? Well, I stayed on and helped with building the ecommerce project. I actually enjoyed working with Jamila, and Paula turned out to be an insightful leader. I learned a lot from her, in fact. For instance, she said that for every event there are three sides that must be taken into account—his side, her side, and then the right side. In the Hiring Committee, I wanted Jeff, Gail wanted Jamila, but Ralph wanted Paula who turned out to be the right person to take the company to the next level.

Paula's leadership style inspired people to bring their best to the table every day. Not only so, she wasn't afraid of people who grew beyond the company, like Jamila, who came to the company as a change-agent and who would move on once the changes were moving in the right direction.

Given all the change—with people leaving and new leadership stepping in—I felt uneasiness within me and decided to take a step back and reevaluate what I really wanted to do. There were a number of people who could have stayed but decided to pursue their own dreams, like Becky. I realized that even though I could manage a project really well, at the end of the day I didn't feel as fulfilled as I did after I finished conducting a seminar or workshop or some other training that helped move people from their Point A to Point B. I also enjoyed putting manuals together and writing.

While I enjoyed my job, it had never been a passion of mine. Getting people from their Point A to Point B was my passion. I knew this was a passion, because after a training or some conference event I would be so juiced and would often say to myself, *Wow, they actually pay me to do this? If I could, I would do this for free.*

After talking it over with Denise, I handed in my notice to Paula who gave me her blessings. She is someone that even today I occasionally check in on to see how she is doing.

So now, I get to follow my passion. The funniest thing about being able to do this is that I actually have Ralph, Paula, and the Hiring Committee to thank for it. Had I not gone through that frustrating and crazy experience, I may never have realized that I should do the very something that I really love and look forward to doing every day.

My purpose in writing this book was primarily to reveal twelve secrets of the Hiring Committee process and to give you insight on how you might approach your own Hiring Committee experience. However, I also want you to realize that there is always tons of behind-the-scenes dynamics going on than you will ever comprehend, much of which you will never know, or understand, or be able to control. But in the end, wherever you end up will be your Point B, or the stepping stone towards your Point B. That's it.

Therefore, relax and go through the process. You will get to where you are supposed to be, if you keep on moving. Enjoy the journey.

NEXT STEPS

Now that these secrets have been revealed to you, I am confident that you will use them to help you get the job that you want. Please allow me to give you these next steps:

1. Leave a review

Okay, so this may not be your necessary next step, but I really would appreciate it if you would do me a favor and leave me a review and let me know what you thought about the material in this book. Your feedback on what you liked or what might be improved would be valuable to me, and it would help me when I next update this material. You can leave a review here (/HIRING-Book).

2. Stay connected

Take a moment to sign up for our GUDEJob newsletter (go to www.gudejob.com and sign up on the home page). When you do I will let you know about updates to this book and will often send you free resources that will help boost your career or move you from your Point A to Point B, so be sure to sign up today. Thanks.

3. Increase your resume response rate

You won't get into the interview until you're selected by potential employers. And potential employers won't select you if you don't connect with them.

And the #1 most powerful way to connect with them is through your resume.

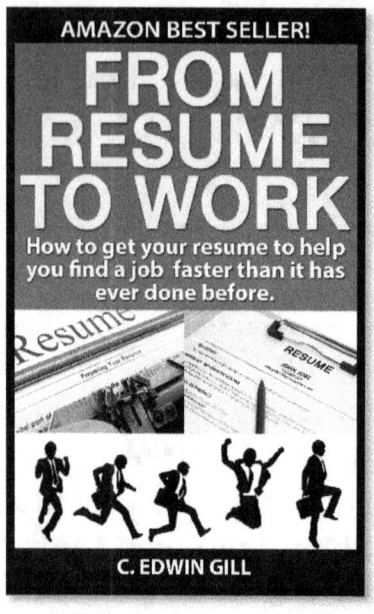

That's why I wrote this book, *From Resume to Work* (**/FRTW-Book**), so that you will learn how to get your resume to connect with employers so that they will want to contact you and offer you an interview.

I discuss new ways that employers test applicants even before the application process, such as putting little instructions in the "How to Apply" section of the job announcement. If applicants follow the instructions completely, Employment Psychologists tell them to place the applicant's resume onto the next steps list. If applicants don't follow instructions, employers are told to reject the resume outright, no matter how good it looks.

If you are sending out tons of resume without getting the response you want, it's most likely that your resume is being rejected for one of the many reasons I discuss in my book.

Therefore, pick up your copy today so that you can get *From Resume to Work.*

4. Get (and keep) the job you want

It's one thing to get a job, yet another to get the job you really want, and yet another thing still to keep the job you really want. I have had a number of Job Information Workshop participants cycle back through the workshops after losing one job and then another. I had to track and assess what was going on with these participants and help them understand why they constantly found themselves unemployed.

 From sitting down with them to resolve this issue, I developed a third book in this series entitled, _First Fired, Last Hired_ (**/FFLH-Book**). What I discovered from the job seekers who came back through our workshops year after year after year, is that they continued to commit the 40 sins of employment that kept them cycling through unemployment. In this book, I share these with you the 40 reasons why these participants didn't have the job that they wanted and what they needed to do about it.

I must warn you that this book is not easy to stomach for many people because—let's face it—who would want to admit that they are guilty of doing things that are keeping them from the job that they want? I sure wouldn't. But in the process of helping thousands of participants understand the things they needed to acknowledge in order to be successful in their careers, I learned a lot about myself which helped me to be successful in my own career.

Therefore, I suggest that you get this book for someone else; or, you can get it so you can go through it to help someone else first. That way, you too can discover and remove obstacles that may be preventing you from moving from your Point A to your Point B.

If you have any questions or comments, please feel free to email me at <u>ed@gudejob.com</u>. Thank you and I appreciate any feedback you would like to share.

THANK YOU

I would like to thank you again for purchasing this book. It is my hope and sincere desire that you will find it helpful and rewarding however you apply it.

I also wanted to remind you to download your free copy of my resource, *How to Become More Valuable* (/More-Valuable). In this free report I will share with you why being valuable is so important (if it isn't important to you already), and how you can go about adding value to others thereby increasing your own value.

I also want to let you know that you can visit our blog www.GudeJob.com/blogs where colleagues and I share strategies and tips on how to find on the job success.

Don't forget to leave a book review on Amazon by going here (/HIRING-Book). This feedback will help me continue to write the kind of books that will help you get results. I really appreciate it. Thank you and have a great day.

C. Edwin Gill

www.ingramcontent.com/pod-product-compliance
Lightning Source LLC
Chambersburg PA
CBHW071302220526
45468CB00001B/235